dog care

Maj. Gen. (Dr.) R.M. Kharb, AVSM has spent nearly four decades breeding, rearing, training and treating dogs. As a young captain of the Remount & Veterinary Corps (RVC) he successfully commanded two Army Dog Units in counter-insurgency operations.

Decorated twice—by the Chief of Army Staff with his commendation medal, and by the President of India on 26 January 1996 with the 'Ati Vishisht Seva Medal'—Maj. Gen. (Dr.) Kharb, AVSM is a fellow of the National Academy of Veterinary Sciences, India.

He also has the singular distinction of introducing a new versatile breed—the Belgian Shepherd—in the Indian Army.

OTHER LOTUS TITLES

Ajit Bhattacharjea	*Sheikh Mohammad Abdullah: Tragic Hero of Kashmir*
Amarinder Singh	*The Last Sunset: The Rise and Fall of the Lahore Durbar*
Anil Dharker	*Icons: Men & Women Who Shaped Today's India*
Aitzaz Ahsan	*The Indus Saga: The Making of Pakistan*
Alam Srinivas & TR Vivek	*IPL: The Inside Story*
Amir Mir	*The True Face of Jehadis: Inside Pakistan's Terror Networks*
Ashok Mitra	*The Starkness of It*
Dr Humanyun Khan & G. Parthasarthy	*Diplomatic Divide*
Gyanendra Pandey & Yunus Samad	*Faultlines of Nationhood*
H.L.O. Garrett	*The Trial of Bahadur Shah Zafar*
Hindustan Times Leadership Summit	*Vision 2020: Challenges for the Next Decade*
M.J. Akbar	*India: The Siege Within*
M.J. Akbar	*The Shade of Swords*
M.J. Akbar	*Byline*
M.J. Akbar	*Blood Brothers: A Family Saga*
Maj. Gen. Ian Cardozo	*Param Vir: Our Heroes in Battle*
Maj. Gen. Ian Cardozo	*The Sinking of INS Khukri: What Happened in 1971*
Madhu Trehan	*Tehelka as Metaphor*
Mushirul Hasan	*India Partitioned. 2 Vols*
Mushirul Hasan	*John Company to the Republic*
Mushirul Hasan	*Knowledge, Power and Politics*
Nayantara Sahgal (ed.)	*Before Freedom: Nehru's Letters to His Sister*
Nilima Lambah	*A Life Across Three Continents*
Robert Hutchison	*The Raja of Harsil: The Legend of Frederick 'Pahari' Wilson*
Sharmishta Gooptu and Boria Majumdar (eds)	*Revisiting 1857: Myth, Memory, History*
Shrabani Basu	*Spy Princess: The Life of Noor Inayat Khan*
Shashi Joshi	*The Last Durbar*
Shashi Tharoor & Shaharyar M. Khan	*Shadows across the Playing Field*
Shyam Bhatia	*Goodbye Shahzadi: A Political Biography*
Thomas Weber	*Gandhi, Gandhism and the Gandhians*
Thomas Weber	*Going Native: Gandhi's Relationship with Western Women*

FORTHCOMING TITLES

Indian Express	*The Prize Stories*
Mohammed Hyder	*October Coup: Memoir of the Struggle for Hyderabad*

foreword Priyanka Gandhi Vadra

dog care
made easy

text Maj. Gen. (Dr.) R.M. Kharb, AVSM

Lotus Collection

First published in 2005
Third impression, 2011

The Lotus Collection
An imprint of
Roli Books Pvt. Ltd
M-75, Greater Kailash II Market,
New Delhi 110 048
Phone: ++91 (011) 4068 2000
Fax: ++91 (011) 2921 7185
E-mail: info@rolibooks.com
Website: www.rolibooks.com
Also at Bangalore, Chennai & Mumbai

Editor: Dipa Chaudhuri
Cover: Sneha Pamneja

Design & Illustrations: Mahendra Sharma
Layout: Narendra Shahi

ISBN: 978-81-7436-351-3

Typeset in bliss-Light by Roli Books Pvt. Ltd and printed at Rakmo Press, Okhla, New Delhi.

~

THIS BOOK IS DEDICATED TO THE MEMORY

OF

MY DAUGHTER DEEPIKA,

MY SON-IN-LAW MAJOR ASHISH KUMAR

AND

THEIR BABY DAUGHTER DEVYANI.

THEY WERE ALL GREAT DOG LOVERS

AND

HAD MOTIVATED ME TO WRITE THIS BOOK.

~

contents

foreword

Thirty-eight years of experience have made Dr. Kharb an expert in understanding the canine world.

In 1989, when I first met him, our dog Toffee had given birth to six puppies. The puppies were about a month old when they began dragging their hindquarters along the floor. Vets of all distinctions were called in—what could the problem be? Someone suggested rickets and prescribed daily Vitamin C injections; another proclaimed that it was a terrible genetic defect.

Dr. Kharb took one look at the bottom-heavy puppies and said matter-of-factly: 'You are feeding them too much. Their stomachs are so full that they can't budge!' It's this sort of simple, pragmatic approach that distinguishes his practice from others. He is also a very patient and caring person.

At about eight weeks, two of our puppies contracted Parvo Virus. As the disease progressed, they became pale shadows of their bright and vivacious selves. We were heartbroken. Each one of us took turns to tend to them. We spent many nights awake by their side; it seemed that they wouldn't pull through. But Dr. Kharb didn't give up hope; he made himself available round the clock. Rushing over to the house at unearthly hours, checking their drips, monitoring their progress or just generally offering support. Both dogs survived the potentially fatal illness and grew into beautiful Retrievers.

With Dr. Kharb's guidance we happily brought up seven dogs at one time. As they grew into healthy adults, it became essential to understand their behaviour in order to care for them properly. Whether it was their playfulness, changes in the tone of their eyes, or their feeding pattern, each was an indicator of their state of being.

Dr. Kharb taught us to read these signs, to deepen our own perception of the complex emotional world of dogs. Most importantly, through him, we learnt and understood that each dog had a distinct personality of his own and needed to be nurtured accordingly.

Over the years I have watched him apply this fundamental understanding in his work as a veterinary surgeon. His compassion as a human being, and his love for dogs is reflected in his profession. Through his years of service, he has had the opportunity to study dogs closely both as individuals and in packs. This has given him an insight into the animal which most dog owners do not have. In his book *Dog Care* he shares the invaluable wisdom he has gained from almost four decades of experience.

I am glad he has undertaken the task of writing this informative and exhaustive manual.

A comprehensive reference such as this is essential for both new owners and tested ones like myself.

Priyanka Gandhi Vadra
Delhi, 2005

preface

I have always been very fond of animals, ever since childhood. I used to pick up stray puppies, bring them home, look after and feed them. This love for animals continued right through my schooldays, which eventually made me join the veterinary college. As a young officer of Remount & Veterinary Corps of the Indian Army, I got a unique opportunity to study the Dog Training Course for officers. There I learnt about canine behaviour and the unique qualities and characteristics of each breed in detail, besides the breeding, rearing, training and care and management of dogs. It was indeed a big boost for my morale and to my interest and love for dogs. Later while commanding the Army Dog Units, I was very impressed by the courage and strength of the canine character and the strong bonding of the dogs with their handlers/trainers.

My association with dogs was further strengthened when I commanded the prestigious President's Body Guard Veterinary Hospital in Delhi. Here I was fortunate enough to interact with many dog lovers who came for advice and asked questions about the care, management and training of their pet dogs. At that time I felt the necessity of a simple ready reckoner on dog care which would provide necessary guidance and answers to commonly asked questions by dog owners.

After my retirement, I decided to put my thoughts and experiences together and write a book on the general care and management of dogs to provide answers to commonly asked questions. *Dog Care* is a tribute to man's best friend for his contribution in improving the quality of human life by his companionship. This book will not only be useful to first-time dog owners but also to others who have pet dogs. They will be able to understand the psychological, emotional and health requirements of their dogs. The book contains separate chapters on care, management, feeding and house training of puppies, adult dogs and elderly dogs. I have included information on choosing the right breed of dogs along with an introduction to common breeds. There is a separate chapter on preventive health care, veterinary first-aid and canine diseases. In order to educate and caution dog owners, there is a separate chapter on diseases transmissible from dogs to human beings. Finally, I have included a chapter on an alternative system of medicine, which includes homeopathy, herbal drugs, acupuncture, acupressure massage and Bach Flower Remedies.

In conclusion, I would like to say that *Dog Care* has been written for those dog lovers who have not owned dogs earlier, and are hesitant or fearful of facing problems connected with dogs. I am sure this book will help in assuaging their doubts and fears about dogkeeping, and will not only provide answers to their questions, but also help in providing better care to their pet dogs, for a healthier and longer life. In a nutshell, *Dog Care* covers almost everything that a dog owner needs to know to enjoy his pet and keep him healthy.

Maj. Gen. (Dr.) R.M. Kharb, AVSM
Delhi, 2005

introduction

The dog in life the finest friend,
First to welcome, foremost to defend,
Whose heart is still his master's own,
Who labours, fights, breathes for him alone.

—Lord Byron

From time immemorial man and dog have had a very close association. When man was a hunter, the dog played a key role as his companion, guard and tracker. He accompanied his master on hunting trips and helped him to find food for his family. Later, when man domesticated other animals, the dog helped him guard and herd them.

With time, the role of the dog vis-à-vis man has changed. Today there are only a few places in the world where a dog is used for herding purposes. But even now, the dog, with his unconditional love and loyalty, is truly man's best friend and companion. Dogs enrich the quality of human life in many ways. With the changing socio-economic scenario, the stresses of day-to-day life, the disintegration of traditional institutions and the rise in crime, humans are looking more towards their pets for emotional comfort and security.

Modern man has utilized the dog's natural gifts of highly developed sense of smell, hearing, loyalty and ferocity to suit his purposes. From the

time of the Romans, dogs have been extensively used for combat duties such as guarding vital defense installations, tracking down infiltrators, detecting explosives and mines, locating enemy ambushes, and rescuing people buried under snow or earthquake rubble, and so on. Trained dogs played a very important role in World War II and thereafter in the wars in Korea and Vietnam, and continue to do so even now in several armies globally.

Recent research conducted on stress management at the State University of New York shows that of all the available antidotes to tension, dogs are the best stress-busters. Even hypersensitive and hyperactive people become calm when in the company of their pet dogs. Dogs like you just as you are. You don't have to live up to their expectations. This kind of unconditional acceptance goes a long way in reducing stress. It has also been proved that stroking and petting your dog reduces blood pressure and pulse rate, and gives you a feeling of well-being. According to a recent study, published in the *Journal of Cardiology*, pet dogs significantly contribute to the recovery of patients suffering from myocardial infarction and other heart diseases. They also help their owners cope with other serious diseases like cancer. The study provides strong evidence that owning a dog improves a person's mental and physical health.

Dogs play an important role in helping physically challenged people. They fulfil the emotional needs of childless couples and elderly people, and are excellent companions for lonely people, making their lives infinitely more meaningful. These animals can be trained to be excellent guard dogs too.

Dogs teach you compassion, calm your nerves, and make you feel better about the world. They don't argue, answer back, cheat or fool you, and are honest and loving. What better companions and

friends could you ask for? Isn't it important then that you provide these wonderful companions with the best possible care?

I have written this book in a question-answer form, to help dog owners find ready answers to commonly asked questions regarding the management, care, discipline and health-related problems of dogs, and enable them to enjoy the companionship of a healthier and more disciplined pet. Also, as dog owners you should be able to administer preliminary first aid to your dog if necessary. However, the advice given on various subjects is not a substitute for the professional advice and services of a veterinarian, who should always be consulted when necessary.

Preparing to Become a Dog Owner

Owning a dog is a joy and a great privilege. However, as a dog owner, you have a serious responsibility and should take care of your pet as best as you can. Dogs have to be fed, groomed, exercised, and taken out several times a day. They are social animals and seek human attention and physical contact. They have to be treated as a part of the family. Therefore, it is essential to be a dog lover and have ample time for your pet before deciding to own a dog.

Having decided to keep a dog, you must select a breed which fits into your lifestyle, and the space available. Each breed has its own characteristics that should be kept in mind while selecting a dog. Through selective cross-breeding, man has created several hundred breeds of dogs in a wide range of shapes and sizes.

The selection of the breed will also depend on why you want to keep a dog. Do you want a dog just as a family pet and companion, or do you also want a guard dog? Some people also have ambitions of owning a show dog.

Before deciding on the breed, you must remember that a puppy continues to grow until about ten months of age. It is therefore important to select a breed that will not be too large for your home when it is fully grown, especially if you live in a flat. You must also keep in mind that larger dogs need more exercise, and it is more expensive to feed and maintain them. Another important consideration is that short-haired dogs need less care as far as grooming is concerned. They also shed less hair in the house!

Nowadays many people want to keep trained guard dogs for security purposes. However, ferocious dogs are dangerous, and you must realize that you cannot keep vicious dogs in civilized society. Dogs that attack people are a serious neighbourhood threat and become liabilities for their owners.

As a matter of fact, smaller breeds are generally more alert and make excellent watchdogs. They need less space and are more economical to maintain. However, choosing a dog is a personal matter, and some people prefer to keep dogs of only one particular breed, irrespective of other considerations.

What is responsible dog ownership?

As a responsible dog owner you must have sufficient time to ensure that your dog has proper meals at the right time; is regularly groomed, exercised and trained; taken to the vet for periodic check-ups, vaccinations, deworming; and above all, provided with companionship and plenty of love.

Which makes for a better pet, a male or a female dog?

This is a matter of personal preference. Female dogs are generally more docile and affectionate. Male dogs tend to be a bit more aggressive than females, and have a tendency to roam, especially when

there are female dogs in season in the vicinity. Female dogs generally come into season (oestrus) twice a year, each season lasting approximately twenty days. At this time they need to be carefully watched and supervised, to prevent unwanted and accidental pregnancies. Spaying (operated upon) your female dog can solve this problem. I would recommend a female dog as a pet.

Is it better to opt for a pure-breed or a mixed-breed puppy?

It is better to get a pure-breed puppy, as it is easy to know with reasonable accuracy what the temperament, size and coat will be like when the puppy grows into an adult. Each breed has its own characteristics, and those of a pure breed will certainly blossom when the puppy becomes a full-grown dog. In comparison, it is not possible to predict what a mixed-breed puppy will be like, though he/she may also grow up to be an intelligent and loving pet.

How much time should you allot daily to look after your dog?

An adult dog needs at least thirty to forty minutes of walking/exercise every day, apart from fifteen to twenty minutes for grooming and feeding twice a day. The dog should be taken out three to four times during the day to urinate and defecate. In addition, there should be time available for regular visits to the vet for check-ups. To impart basic obedience training, at least thirty to forty minutes are required daily for a three to four months.

What approximate expenditure is involved in the upkeep of a small, medium and large dog?

The average monthly expenditure for the food, upkeep and health care of a well-maintained dog is:

Small breed: Rs 500-700

Medium breed: Rs 700-1000

Large breed: Rs 1000-1500

Additionally, vaccinations/deworming costs are approximately Rs 1000 per year.

The expenditure on dog equipment, depending on its quality, varies between Rs 500-1000 annually.

Obedience training costs Rs 2500-3000 per month if the dog requires it.

Selecting the Right Breed

It is beyond the scope of this book to describe all the breeds of dogs. However, the characteristics of some of the popular, common breeds are given briefly. For the purpose of classification, dogs are categorized into three main groups: small, medium and large.

Small Breeds: Chihuahua, Spitz, Pug, Lhasa Apso, Cocker Spaniel, Pomeranian, Dachshund, Pekingese, Poodle (toy), French Bulldog, Miniature Pinscher and Papillon.

Medium Breeds: Labrador, Boxer, Bulldog, Bull Terrier, Samoyed, Beagle, Whippet, Dalmatian, Basset Hound, Saluki, Keeshond, Schnauzer, Pointer, Himalayan Sheepdog (Bhutia), Rampur Hound, Foxhound, Corgi and Basenji.

Large Breeds: German Shepherd (Alsatian), Dobermann, Rottweiler,

Golden Retriever, Great Dane, St. Bernard, Bull Mastiff, Pyrenean Mountain Dog, Bloodhound, Afghan Hound, Collie, Belgian Shepherd Dog, Irish Wolfhound, Tibetan Mastiff, Greyhound, Rhodesian Ridgeback and Newfoundland.

Which are the five most popular small-breed dogs in India? What are their characteristics?

The five most popular breeds in India are Spitz, Lhasa Apso, Cocker Spaniel, Dachshund and Pekingese.

Spitz: They are generally white in colour, with long hair, curled, bushy tails, and pricked ears. Smaller replicas of Samoyeds, people not familiar with dog breeds commonly know Spitz as Poms. They are good watchdogs, as they do not make friends with strangers easily and tend to be a bit temperamental. Their long coats require extra care and regular brushing.

Lhasa Apsos: Commonly available Lhasa Apsos are long-haired, small-sized dogs, originally from Tibet, and are generally black and white, or fawn in colour. Their bushy tails are curled and rest on their backs, and the long hair from their foreheads cover their faces and eyes. Lhasa Apsos make good watchdogs. Some Apsos are temperamental and tend to be snappy. Their long-haired coats need regular brushing. They weigh between eight to twelve kilograms, and their height is between ten and twelve inches.

Cocker Spaniels: They make ideal pets. One of the most popular breeds, they are very friendly, adaptable and fond of outdoor life. Endowed with an excellent sense of smell, Cocker Spaniels are used as sniffer dogs and also for hunting, flushing out and retrieving birds. Their long ears and prominent foreheads make them look very innocent and adorable, and they are very good with children. As a breed they are docile and do not attack or snap at people. They need regular grooming

BEAGLE

COCKER SPANIEL

DALMATIAN

DOBERMANN PINSCHER

FOX TERRIER

GREAT DANE

GOLDEN RETRIEVER

GERMAN SHEPHERD

DACHSHUND

ST. BERNARD

HIMALAYAN SHEEP DOG (Gaddi)

LABRADOR

LHASA APSO

PEKINGESE

POMERANIAN

PUG

ROTTWEILER

SPITZ

BOXER

BASSET HOUND

and care for their ears, however. Periodic professional cleaning of the ears by a vet is desirable. They weigh between twelve and fifteen kilograms, and are fourteen to sixteen inches tall.

Dachshunds: A very popular German breed, Dachshunds have long bodies and short legs, and are normally black with tan markings, although brown and liver-chestnut are also common colours. They possess good tracking noses and the loud bark of hounds. With temperaments as bold as terriers, Dachshunds are very affectionate and excellent as watchdogs. They are a hardy, brave breed and make excellent pets. Their short coats are ideally suited for Indian climatic conditions. Dachshunds come in two sizes—standard and miniature. The length of their bodies is almost three times that of their height at the shoulders. On an average they weigh between eight and fourteen kilograms.

Terriers: Terriers comprise a group of several different breeds, such as Bull Terriers, Fox Terriers, Scottish Terriers, Tibetan Terriers, Skye Terriers, Airedale Terriers, Australian Terriers, Kerry Blue Terriers, and many more. But they have certain common traits—boldness, strength and high spirits. Most Terriers make good watchdogs, though some tend to be over-aggressive. Some breeds have been used for hunting. Most Terriers have long hair and need regular grooming and care of their coats. Their height and weight varies; some, such as the Australian and the Skye Terriers, are very small.

Which of the small dogs make the best pets and are also good watchdogs?

A lot depends on personal choice, but keeping Indian climatic conditions in mind, I would strongly recommend Dachshunds and the Spitz.

What is the difference between a Pomeranian, Spitz and Samoyed?

People sometimes get confused between a Spitz, Pomeranian and Samoyed. Though these breeds are similar in appearance, they differ in size. Pomeranians are the smallest and are actually a toy breed, generally golden in colour. The Spitz is bigger than the Pomeranian, but smaller than the Samoyed. The Spitz belongs to the small-dog category, whereas the Samoyed is medium-sized. The Spitz and Samoyeds are both generally white and have a close resemblance as far as their general appearance is concerned.

Amongst medium-sized dogs, which are the five most popular breeds in India?

In the medium-sized range, the most popular breeds are Labradors, Boxers, Dalmatians, Himalayan Sheepdogs and Bull Terriers.

Could you specify the main characteristics of Labradors?

Labradors are the most popular family dogs in the medium-sized category, and make excellent and reliable pets. With amiable natures, intelligent, gentle and good-tempered, they are exceptionally dependable. They are easy to train, and not much effort is required to look after their short coats. They are generally black or golden in colour, constitutionally strong and active, with a lot of stamina. Retrieving is in their genes, so they make excellent gun dogs. They love playing in water and are good swimmers. This breed is very adaptable in its feeding habits and is willing to accept any kind of food. Labradors have very highly developed senses of smell and hearing and are commonly used for sniffing, tracking, and as guide dogs for the blind.

Do Labradors make good watchdogs?

Though Labradors are very friendly, and always eager to please, they do guard against intruders.

Are Labradors suitable for keeping in flats? What is their average size and weight?

A sporting breed, Labradors are best suited to spacious houses. However, if taken out every day for a three or four kilometre walk, and allowed some regular play in an open area, they can adapt to living in a flat very well. On an average they are about twenty-two to twenty-three inches in height and twenty-eight to thirty-two kilograms in weight.

What is your opinion of Boxers?

Boxers are almost as good as Labradors. They are well known for their courage and make excellent guard dogs. They are affectionate, playful and good with children. Athletic and always keen to walk and play, Boxers use their paws in a punchy fighting style while playing.

If guarding is the main purpose, which of the medium-sized dogs would you recommend?

Boxers are ideal for the purpose, as besides their natural guarding instincts, they look ferocious. However, other good guard dogs in the medium-sized segment are Bull Terriers, Dalmatians, Himalayan Sheepdogs and Samoyeds.

Which are the five most popular breeds in the large-dog segment?

Alsatians, Golden Retrievers, Dobermann Pinschers, Great Danes and Rottweilers are the most popular large breeds.

Which amongst the large dogs is the most popular breed and why?

Alsatians (German Shepherd Dogs) are extremely intelligent, and the most popular in the large-dog segment. They are the most versatile dogs in the world. Besides being popular family dogs, Alsatians are used by the police and the armed forces for guarding, protecting, tracking and rescuing; and as sniffer dogs and guide dogs for the physically challenged. With correct and early training they can be obedient and loyal companions.

How would you rate Dobermanns as pets?

Dobermanns are also a popular breed in the large-dog segment. They are very intelligent, athletic and powerful and are widely used for guarding, tracking and as watchdogs. Their athletic bodies allow them to run very fast. However, they are a bit headstrong and sometimes overly aggressive, and it takes time to discipline them.

Golden Retriever is also a popular breed amongst large dogs. What are its main characteristics?

There is no doubt that Golden Retrievers are becoming more popular as pets because of their friendly, gentle and affectionate disposition. They have a regal appearance with their silky golden coats. True to their name, they are good retrievers. However, their long coats require regular grooming and maintenance. They are a hardy breed and often turn out to be excellent watchdogs, but by and large, on account of their good nature, they are friendly with strangers.

Rottweilers are reported to be dangerous dogs. Would you recommend them as pets?

Rottweilers are strong, bold and courageous dogs. Trained Rottweilers make excellent guard dogs and are used in the armed forces. They are affectionate with their masters, ideal companions and guard dogs. However, like Dobermanns, some Rottweilers can be over-aggressive and a threat if not properly trained. They can attack suddenly on the sly, without giving any warning signs, and are often unpredictable. Therefore, they are not suitable as family pets. Some countries have passed a legislation banning the breeding of Rottweilers.

These days we often see people with St. Bernards in India. What are their characteristics, and do they acclimatize to our tropical conditions easily?

St. Bernards originated in the St. Bernard Pass in the Alps, where they are used as pathfinders and rescue dogs. They are usually friendly and affectionate, and their melancholic eyes make them look very innocent and lovable. St. Bernards make good pets, but they have a large appetite as well, in keeping with their size. As such, they are expensive to maintain. They suffer in the heat, and are not very comfortable during the summer.

Do Great Danes make good pets?

Great Danes are kings amongst dogs. This giant breed was evolved specially for hunting tusked wild boars. They are gentle, affectionate and physically suited for spacious living, but adapt themselves very well to apartments. Majestic and strong, they make excellent guard dogs as their size and carriage have a deterring effect on any intruder. Great Danes make wonderful pets if one can afford their cost and maintenance, and exercise them adequately.

Is it true that there are basic fundamental differences in the physiology of small and large dogs?

There are a number of fundamental differences in the physiology of small and large breeds, as summarized below:

- The age when dogs mature varies. Small breeds often mature early (at the age of eight or nine months), whereas larger

breeds take longer to mature (generally twelve to eighteen months).

- Their growth rate in body weight is also variable. Small-breed full-grown dogs may attain twenty times their birth weight, but large-breed full-grown dogs may ultimately be a hundred times their weight at birth.
- The weight-wise energy requirement of smaller dogs is almost twice that of larger breeds.
- The weight of the digestive tract vis-à-vis the total body weight in small breeds is about 7 per cent of the body weight, whereas in larger breeds it is about 2.7 per cent. When the volume of ingested food is too much, the stomachs of larger breeds distort and twist, resulting in stomach dilation and bloating. This can have serious consequences, and hence, very large meals should never be given to dogs of large breeds.
- The life expectancy of larger and heavier breeds of dogs is much shorter than that of smaller breeds.

If a dog were used mainly as a guard dog, which breed would you recommend?

The German Shepherd makes the best guard dog. However, if well trained, Boxers, Dalmatians, Himalayan Sheepdogs, Dobermanns, Rottweilers, Belgian Shepherd Dogs and Great Danes are also good for this purpose.

Checklist for Choosing the Right Breed:

- Availability of space is important and should be kept in mind—smaller breeds for apartments and larger breeds for large houses.
- Big dogs are more expensive to maintain than smaller breeds.

- A family with children should opt for friendly breeds, like Cocker Spaniels and Labradors.
- Elderly people should keep smaller or medium-sized dogs that are alert and make good watchdogs, such as Dachshunds, Spitz, Boxers and Dalmatians.
- For a single owner, a dog with a calm temperament (one that will not mind being left alone), such as a Cocker Spaniel or Labrador, is ideal.
- Long-haired breeds, such as Lhasa Apsos, need more grooming and constantly shed their hair. This should be kept in mind.
- German Shepherds, Dobermanns, Dalmatians and Boxers make good guard dogs.
- For the security of houses/farmhouses in remote and lonely areas, a small dog such as a Dachshund, Spitz or Lhasa Apso should be kept inside the house, and two bigger dogs such as German Shepherds, Rottweilers or Dobermanns should be kept outside in the compound.

Basic Canine Characteristics

Wolves and dogs share a common ancestry, and while the former retained their wildness and ferocity, the latter became tractable and domesticated. However, there are several similarities between the two. They have the same period of gestation and a strong pack instinct. They can be cross-bred with each other to produce offspring. They also suffer from the same parasitic diseases. Both love to eat foul-smelling, rotten flesh, and roll in it to mask their own body odour. Both wag their tails in pleasure and tuck them between their hind legs when frightened. They curl their lips into a snarl when angry and

use scent-marked pathways, with their urine deposited in strategic positions, to signal their presence in the area. They communicate with body language and odour. Experienced dog owners know and understand all of this. It is very important for prospective owners to know about how dogs use these unique ways of communication. Like their wolf relatives, dogs have a highly developed sense of smell, sight and hearing. They also have a refined sense of touch. These have helped the dog survive, and differentiate between friends and foes.

What is pack behaviour?

Like their wolf relatives, dogs are compelled by a unique instinct to hunt and walk together. Stray dogs living in secure domesticated conditions in rural areas live and hunt together. In the absence of other dogs, pet dogs look upon humans (family members) as members of their pack. They respect their human leader—a trait similar to that of pack behaviour.

Some dogs have destructive behavioural traits. What is the reason for this and how does one overcome this problem?

Growing dogs generally exhibit this type of behaviour. They pick up objects playfully and can do a lot of damage. As they grow older, most of them outgrow these traits. However, certain dogs, when left alone in the house, feel stressed and resort to destroying objects. They may also howl and bark continually. Dogs also tend to behave this way due to a lack of adequate exercise. To overcome this problem they must be checked with the stern command 'NO' when found indulging in this kind of behaviour. Adequate daily exercise is essential, and as far as possible, dogs should not be left alone in the house.

What is the importance of socializing/introducing one's dog to other dogs?

It is good for dogs to meet other healthy dogs (preferably of the same age group), and play with them in a park or open area. If they do this they became more tolerant of other dogs and do not get overexcited on seeing a new dog. It is also good to allow puppies to indulge in play-fighting. However, you should never allow puppies or dogs to play or come in contact with stray or sick dogs, as they can contract serious infections from them.

Is it true that a dog's sense of smell is more developed than his other senses?

It is a fact that a dog's sense of smell is very highly developed—it is forty to forty-five times more acute than that of human beings. This is due to the fact that dogs have 225 million receptor cells in their nasal mucosa, compared to only 5 million in the case of human beings. Dog owners know that their pets use their noses all the time to investigate new objects, other dogs and unknown people. When two dogs meet, they try and sniff each other's genitals, to ascertain each other's sex and state of mind. Man has utilized their highly developed sense of smell to detect explosives, mines and narcotics, and to track down thieves and infiltrators. Dogs are also used to detect enemy ambushes and people buried in avalanches and earthquakes.

What does scent-marking and scent-signalling mean?

All dogs urinate at strategic locations to mark their territory. The scent of the secretion of special glands called anal glands, which is passed out with the stool, serves the same purpose—it sends a clear signal to other dogs about how long ago the depositor of the stool or urine passed through that area.

Do dogs have a better-developed sense of hearing than humans?

A dog's sense of hearing is highly developed—almost twenty times more than that of human beings. They can hear ultra-high-frequency sounds with notes up to 35 KHz. This is an evolutionary adaptation which helps them hunt. That is why they can accurately detect the sound of their owners' car, and their footsteps from a long distance, and give advance warning of their arrival. Amazingly, they can differentiate between the sounds of car engines of similar makes or models, and the footsteps of known people, from a long distance.

Is it true that dogs have better vision than human beings?

Dogs can see better than humans in poor light conditions due to the predominance of rod receptors in their retinas.

Why do a dog's eyes get a greenish or yellowish-green colour at night when lit up by the headlights of a vehicle or a torch?

This is because of the reflective layer, tapetum, at the back of their eyes.

Do dogs have a sixth sense?

Many owners are convinced that their dogs can sense their feelings of joy and sorrow. They also provide advance warning when children are approaching home after school, and howl in a peculiar fashion to warn of the impending death of a person.

Is it true that dogs have the ability to warn us in advance about natural calamities such as earthquakes?

Yes, it is true. Scientific evidence also supports the view that dogs have an electromagnetic sense, which makes them sensitive to earth tremors and vibrations. They howl in a strange manner in groups just before an earthquake.

Do dogs have the ability to sniff and diagnose human ailments?

Dogs are being trained in the West to sniff patients and diagnose diseases such as diabetes and cancer. However, this research is still in its experimental stage.

Why do dogs curl up their bodies while sleeping?

Curling up conserves their body heat, and they also feel more secure in this position.

Can dogs see in the dark and differentiate between colours?

Dogs can see in relatively poor light because they have more rods in their retinas than human beings. However, they have poor colour vision as they have a fewer number of cones.

Why do dogs drag their hindquarters on the ground or lick their anus?

They do this to relieve the anal glands located on both sides of their

anus, which sometimes get impacted, and to relieve the irritation caused by intestinal worms.

Why do dogs scratch the ground after urinating?

This is to mark their territory and to provide evidence of their recent presence at that particular spot to o'

Why do dogs gulp their food instead of chewing it?

Eating as quickly as possible is a pattern of behaviour inherited from wolves. In the wild, after making a kill, wolves are vulnerable to an attack on their prey by other predators. That is why they eat very fast. This habit is ingrained in dogs too, and like their ancestors, they also wolf down their food.

Why do dogs dig holes in the ground/lawn?

This is another remnant of their ancestry. Wolves dig holes in the ground to bury excess food. Sometimes dogs also dig holes to bury bones or food.

Why do pet dogs bark so loudly when strangers come to the house or even approach it?

This is part and parcel of the pack instinct inherited by dogs from wolves. Pet dogs consider themselves to be members of the pack (the family they belong to), and the house is the most important part of the pack's territory. Therefore, when it is about to be invaded by strangers, they start barking to warn the other members of the pack (family) about the intrusion.

Why do puppies chase their tails?

Recently weaned puppies that have been separated from their littermates sometimes do this. They are probably unable to identify their tails as a part of their own bodies. However, they soon get out of this habit.

Do dogs use their ears to communicate?

Yes, they do, especially those with floppy ears. Confident dogs keep their ears in a forward position, whereas dogs under threat from dominant rivals draw their ears back tightly against the side of their heads.

Do dogs use their tails to communicate?

A raised tail indicates alertness and possible challenge, and one held low between the hind legs is a gesture of submission.

Why are some dogs more aggressive than others?

Dogs have been traditionally reared to guard and to fight other dogs. It is because of these combative genes that some dogs are very aggressive.

Are dogs jealous?

Yes, they are, especially when new people or other pets are introduced into the household. They find they are not getting the kind of attention they are used to, and usually become depressed, and in some cases, aggressive. Sometimes they may defecate or urinate inside the house

out of jealousy. In order to overcome this problem, you would need to pay more attention, give more playtime, and take your dog for longer walks. In due course, your pet will accept the new addition to the family.

Are dogs able to find their way back home from an unfamiliar area or long distances?

Dogs have the ability of finding their way back home from hundreds of miles away, due to their electromagnetic ability. Often pet dogs that are stolen manage to walk back home even after several months, surprising their owners.

What are dogs trying to communicate when they paw you?

Pawing at humans is an affectionate gesture, and dogs want you to interact or play with them. Pawing at the door either indicates that they want to go out to answer the call of nature, or that they want to leave the room.

Do dogs have a highly developed sense of taste?

The sense of taste in dogs is very closely linked with their sense of smell. An appetizing smell stimulates their taste buds, and they begin to salivate and dribble. Otherwise, dogs have far fewer taste buds than humans. Therefore, it is important, when feeding dogs, to concentrate on the flavour of their meal rather than its contents. An ordinary meal of rice and vegetables can be made more palatable by adding some meat broth or soup to it.

Do dogs like to be petted?

Yes, dogs appreciate human contact. They love to be cuddled and petted by their owners, and show their affection by licking their hands and faces, and also by pawing them and sitting on their laps.

Psychologically, what is the effect of the human touch on dogs?

As in the case of humans, dogs feel secure and wanted when cuddled and petted. This also has a positive effect on their behaviour and temperament.

What are the signs when a dog is likely to attack or bite?

The body language of dogs indicates whether they will attack or bite. Making direct contact with the eyes, they assume an aggressive pose, snarling or baring their teeth and growling, and the hair on their backs stands up.

What should one do when faced with aggressive dogs?

Do not run away. Stand still and keep looking into their eyes. Do not show fear. Talk to them politely from a distance, trying to pacify them. If this does not succeed, then pretend to pick up a stone from the ground. This will scare them off.

Why do male dogs lift their hind legs while urinating?

Male dogs do this after they have attained sexual maturity, that is, after nine to ten months of age; this is connected to scent-marking. In this way, they are able to spray their urine over a large area and mark their territory, informing other dogs of their presence. Some female dogs also do this sometimes for the same reason.

Why do dogs sometimes roll on ground that emanates an odour of rotten flesh?

This strange trait has been inherited from their wolf ancestors, presumably to mask their own body odour by a stronger smell, so that they can hunt undetected by their prey.

What precautions should one take to avoid the problem of aggressive behaviour when rearing puppies?

A few simple rules must be observed to ensure that puppies do not develop aggressive patterns of behaviour towards members of the family. It is important that the whole family, including children old enough to give commands, exerts its authority over the puppies, so that they grow up assuming a position subordinate to the people in the house. This is most important while rearing puppies of more assertive breeds such as Dobermanns and Rottweilers, and also male puppies. Do not over-pamper the puppies. Give rewards and treats only when they obey your commands. According to research on animal behaviour, dogs are just as happy being subordinate members of the pack (family), as they are in a more dominant role. Aggressive behaviour in puppies, such as growling or snapping, needs to be punished immediately in order to subdue it. Socializing with other dogs and obedience training are also strongly recommended to suppress aggressive behaviour. If these tendencies continue, owners should seek the assistance of their vet or a professional dog trainer.

What is fear biting or fear aggression in puppies or dogs, and how does one overcome it?

Fear biting has its roots in early unpleasant experiences. It is natural for dogs to be fearful of strange stimuli and react aggressively to situations that evoke anxiety or fear. For example, if puppies are raised without any exposure to children, children may produce a reaction of fear and the dog's natural response would be to bark, growl or snap at them. One must habituate young dogs to fear-evoking stimuli through repeated exposure to such situations. If the puppies seem afraid of children, they should be introduced to them in a friendly and casual manner. It is more difficult to train or habituate older dogs to overcome fear stimuli. Young puppies should be repeatedly exposed to vacuum

cleaners, lawn mowers, bicycle riders, thunder, crackers, cars and veterinary clinics, so that they become used to them.

How can you train puppies to stay alone in the house? Can separation anxiety be avoided?

Leave the puppies alone for a short time, and reward them with a food treat afterwards. Gradually increase the duration of separation and make much of them when you return. Training puppies is much easier than correcting the problem in adult dogs.

Essential Dog Equipment

It is important to procure some essential canine equipment before bringing a puppy into your house. Puppies need a bed of their own, food and water bowls, appropriate grooming equipment, a neck collar and leash, and toys to play with.

The following are essential:

PLASTIC BASKET

A plastic basket as a bed: A plastic basket is preferable to a cane one as it is difficult to chew and easier to clean. The basket should be fitted with a washable mattress. A foam mattress makes an ideal bed for grown-up dogs as it is soft, light and retains body heat. It is also easy to wash.

FEEDING & WATER BOWLS

Food and water bowls: Stainless steel food bowls are best, and ceramic bowls are ideally suited for keeping water.

Grooming equipment appropriate for the dog's coat: There are rubber, bristle (with hard and soft bristles) and wire brushes and steel combs. The type of brush required will depend on whether your dog has short or long hair. A rubber brush loosens dead hair and dirt, while one with bristles removes them along with the debris. A wire brush is useful for untangling hair.

BRUSHES & COMBS

Collar and leash: Depending on the size and age of the dog, nylon or leather collars and leashes should be procured. Nylon leashes and collars are better suited for puppies as they are softer, cheaper and easier to maintain than leather leashes. Nylon is also much stronger than leather and is not affected by regular washing.

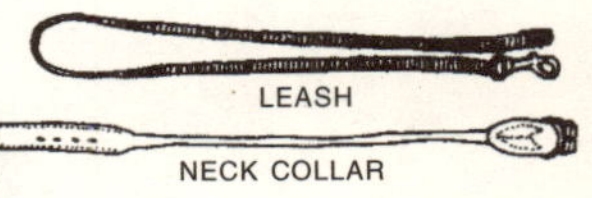

LEASH

NECK COLLAR

Muzzle: This is required for puppies or dogs to prevent them from biting or eating rubbish. It is also helpful in controlling dogs during veterinary examinations. The muzzle can be plastic or leather.

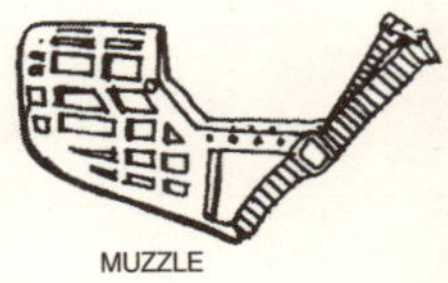

MUZZLE

Toys: Dogs love toys such as tennis balls, dumb-bells, frisbees, soft toys which squeak, chewy rubber toys and bones, and so on.

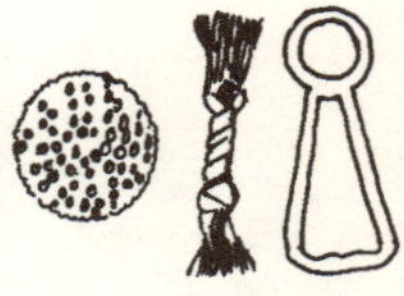

TOYS

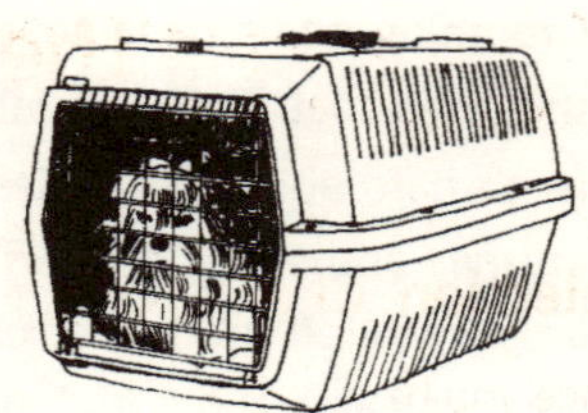
PORTABLE KENNEL

A portable plastic kennel or puppy pen: This is helpful when house-training a puppy or travelling with your dog.

Dog coat: A dog coat or sweater is required during the winter months.

Clippers: Coat clippers are required to clip the hair of long-haired dogs, and nail clippers to trim their nails periodically.

Scissors: A pair of scissors is required for trimming matted hair.

1

the puppy

Selection of a Puppy

Once you have decided the breed you want, you have taken a major step in selecting your dog. The next step is locating the source and choosing the right puppy. In India, it is customary to get a puppy from the litter of a friend's dog. However, a number of professional dog breeders advertise the sale of puppies in newspapers, though some have only specific breeds. It is advisable to get a puppy from a reliable source, where you can see the parents, especially the mother, and check their temperament, so that you have a better idea what the puppy will be like as an adult, in both physical attributes and temperament. Buying puppies from pet shops or breeders who cannot show you the parents is a risky proposition, as there are many unscrupulous people around who want to make easy money by selling puppies of questionable purity and temperament.

Having located the source, the next step is to choose the right puppy from the litter. Ask for all the puppies to be taken out on a lawn or an open area, and observe them at play for some time from a distance. It is easier to judge a puppy's temperament when he is with companions. Eliminate the shy and the bad-tempered ones. Choose one from those that seem balanced in temperament, healthy, bright, alert and lively. Your final selection, however, should depend on the advice of your vet, particularly if you have never owned a dog before. Deciding on a male or female puppy is a matter of personal preference, as both males and females have plus and minus points.

At what age should one procure a puppy?

Puppies should stay with their mother until they are eight weeks old. However, most breeders in India give away or sell puppies when they are five to six weeks old. You should try and persuade the breeder to let the puppy stay with his mother till he is eight weeks old. However, it is possible to rear a six-week-old puppy.

Are cross-breeds or mongrels less intelligent than pure-breed dogs?

Cross-breeds or mongrels are as intelligent as pure-breed dogs and make excellent pets. They are hardier and have a stronger constitution.

What are the signs of good health that one should look for in a puppy?

A healthy puppy is active, alert, playful, with clear bright eyes, and no nasal discharge. The coat should be shining, soft and lustrous, without any dandruff. There should be no ectoparasites such as ticks or fleas. The gums should be pink, and the ears clean, without any odour or discharge. There should be no visible deformity of the limbs and the legs should appear straight. The anal region should be clean and dry (with no signs of diarrhoea), and there should be no discharge from the genital region.

Should one opt only for a pure-breed and Kennel Club-registered puppy vis-à-vis a cross-breed?

Opting for a puppy born of pedigreed and Kennel Club-registered

parents is a wise decision, as you get to know the ultimate size, shape and temperament of the dog. Your puppy will bear a close resemblance to his parents and will possess the characteristics of the breed, guaranteed by selective breeding. If you are interested in breeding your dog, you should keep a pedigreed and Kennel Club-registered puppy. The price of such a puppy is definitely much higher than that of a non-registered pure-bred. It is not possible to predict the ultimate size, coat length and temperament of a mixed-breed puppy, so keeping one is a bit of a gamble.

What else should be kept in mind when selecting a puppy?

Availability of space is important. People living in flats should opt for puppies of smaller breeds, while those living in spacious houses have a choice, and can keep a larger dog. Budget considerations are also important. Smaller breeds cost less, and maintaining them is less expensive than large breeds, which require more exercise, food and living space. With children in the family, it is better to choose a friendly breed such as a Cocker Spaniel or Labrador. Generally, medium and larger-sized breeds are more tolerant of rough handling by children, and make better playmates. Elderly people should keep small or medium-sized breeds, which are easy to train and look after. Also remember that dogs with long hair need frequent grooming, and also shed hair, which means more work for the owner and his family.

What is a reasonable price for a healthy puppy?

There is a wide range in the price of puppies. Some of the smallest breeds, such as pure-bred Pomeranians, Pekingese and Chihuahuas, have the highest price tags. Highly pedigreed puppies of any breed are expensive, ranging between Rs 10,000-15,000. However, a healthy, pedigreed puppy of a common breed should cost between

Rs 5,000-8,000. Pure-breed puppies, not registered with the Kennel Club, and without pedigree certificates, are available for Rs 2,500 to Rs 3,000.

There are several Kennel Clubs in India. Which is the most authentic and reliable?

The KCI (Kennel Club of India) is the main one, with its headquarters at Chennai. It is affiliated with the Kennel Club of London and is internationally recognized. However, there are several regional Kennel Clubs, which are affiliated to KCI. While buying a registered puppy, remember to collect the registration certificate and the transfer of registration form, duly signed by the breeder.

Do pedigreed puppies need more care than mixed-breed ones?

All puppies need the same care, whether they are pure-breeds or mongrels. As a puppy owner you should treat your puppy as though he is the best puppy in the world.

Is pedigree a guarantee of good health?

Pedigree gives detailed information about the parentage of the puppy. It is not a guarantee of good health.

Basic Puppy Care and Feeding

Having got a puppy, you should take him to your vet for a general check-up. Your vet will also advise you about immunization shots, deworming, the feeding schedule and house-training, if you are not too familiar with how to bring up a puppy. You should also clear any doubts you may have about how to take care of the puppy. The vet will make a health-record card for the puppy, indicating your next appointment with him, and may also prescribe multivitamin drops, a calcium tonic, and any other supplement he feels is necessary.

The next step is bringing the puppy home. Most puppies are a little frightened in totally new surroundings, and need reassurance on their arrival. Make sure that you give the puppy a lot of affection so that the trauma of separation from the mother and littermates is reduced. The puppy will take some time to settle down (about a week). Food and water bowls should be kept at a convenient place. They should be heavy enough to remain stationary while the puppy is eating or drinking, and should have straight sides so that the food is not pushed over the edge to the floor.

The puppy should initially be fed the same food he was having at the breeders, and the new diet schedule should be introduced gradually. Soon after the puppy's arrival, give him some diluted milk, after which he ought to be left in the lawn, balcony or veranda to urinate or defecate.

Nutrition is the key factor in promoting good health and longevity. It is also an important part of the management of many diseases. During the first six months the puppy grows rapidly. Without the correct nutrients, his body will not be able to build and repair vital organs, muscles, bones and immune defenses, thus adversely affecting his growth. On the other hand, consumption of too much of certain nutrients can predispose your puppy or dog to certain diseases. It is important that the diet contains an adequate amount of quality protein, fat, carbohydrate, vitamins and minerals. However, different dogs have different nutritional needs.

This is also the time to give your puppy a short name. Make sure you use only that name always.

Provide a comfortable bed for your puppy, preferably in an enclosed pen. If a pen is not available, a cardboard box with a lid and holes all around for proper ventilation will do. During the winter months, the bed should provide protection from draughts.

What preparations should be made before bringing the puppy home?

Before bringing the puppy home you should ready a bed, food and water bowls, and a grooming kit appropriate for his coat. Baby foods such as Cerelac or Farex should also be bought. Select a small room where the puppy will be kept. Also arrange for a puppy pen made of wire net, open at the top and approximately two feet high. Place a small bed inside the pen. This can be plastic or cane, with bedding of some washable material. An adequate number of newspaper sheets should be used to cover the floor of the pen to soak up the urine. A few rubber toys for the puppy to play with and chew on should also be there. A hot-water bottle will be required to keep the puppy warm during the winter months. If it is not possible to get an open wire-net pen, modify a wooden or cardboard box. Take adequate precautions to provide a safe environment for the puppy in the house, as all puppies are inquisitive, and they tend to eat anything, which can cause serious problems. Most accidents are preventable; you should ensure that the puppy does not have access to strings, small balls (such as golf balls), sponges, plastic foil, anti-freeze coolants, rat traps and exposed electrical cords.

Is it true that almost all puppies cry when left alone at night? What should one do in such a situation?

Weaning and separating the puppy from his mother and siblings is a traumatic experience for him. All puppies cry when left alone, especially at night. This is normal. A hot-water bottle wrapped in a towel on his bed during winter and a loud ticking clock will comfort him. Ensure that he is adequately protected from cold and draughts, and has a fan or cooler during the summer months. Do not bring a crying puppy to

your bedroom or bed. Ignore the crying, provided it is not due to the cold or an empty stomach. The puppy will settle down in due course. In extreme cases, when the whining and crying is unbearable, you can shift his pen or box next to your bed and gently fondle his head with your hand till he stops crying.

What food should be given to the puppy on his arrival and how often should one feed him?

Follow the breeder's directions and menu for the first few days. The puppy should be fed four to five times a day at this stage. After a few days, change the diet, with advice from your vet, to one which suits your convenience. Include eggs, milk, bread, rice, vegetables and meat in it.

What is the best food for a puppy?

Puppies need a high-energy diet to meet the requirements of rapid growth. The food must be easily digestible, with enough proteins and fats to ensure a supply of optimum energy. In India, most puppies are reared on fresh food prepared at home. The only problem with fresh food is that it can lead to nutritional deficiencies, causing stunted growth or bone deformities due to a mismatched calcium-to-phosphorus ratio. Some well-reputed canine breeders use commercial food specially prepared for puppies, which are more balanced and meet the exact nutritional requirement of the dog. Having selected the right puppy food, follow the feeding schedule according to the instructions on the label. In order to avoid nutritional deficiencies, you must take your vet's advice if you are feeding fresh food to your puppy.

Do puppies drink water?

Water is as essential for a puppy as it is for a fully-grown dog. A water bowl with plenty of fresh water should always be available. However, since freshly prepared food and milk contain some water, the quantity of water required in the winter months decreases. It increases during the summer months and when the puppy is suffering from diarrhoea. Dehydration in puppies can be life-threatening, as the living cells of the body cannot exist without water.

Should one give milk to a puppy?

In India, puppies are normally weaned when they are five to six weeks old. Their mother's milk is different in composition from that of the cow or buffalo. Therefore, giving them milk after they have been weaned is likely to cause diarrhoea. Feed your puppy small quantities of milk diluted with water (three parts of milk to one part of water), and if he adjusts to it, gradually increase the quantity of milk, eventually stop mixing water in it. However, if the puppy gets diarrhoea, try a dilution of fifty per cent milk with fifty per cent water. Milk products such as cottage cheese are good for puppies.

How do you feed puppies that are indifferent eaters?

Over-indulgent owners who pamper their puppies with table scraps and titbits all the time are mainly responsible for creating fussy eaters. Such puppies lose interest in their normal food. They are clever and know that tastier food awaits them if they wait and do not eat their normal food. Therefore, do not give treats or table scraps to your puppy.

How do you know if you are feeding your puppy a sufficient amount of food?

The amount of food required by a puppy varies with age, breed, size and level of activity. Commercially-marketed puppy foods are prepared

according to the body weight of the puppy. Record the puppy's weight initially at fortnightly intervals and after that at monthly intervals, till the puppy is nine months old. The thumb rule is to let the puppy eat as much as he/she wants in fifteen minutes, and then remove the feeding bowl.

Should the puppy be fed hot or cold food?

The food should be slightly warm.

Specimen Puppy Diet

From the age of six weeks to three months (four meals a day):

Morning (7.30 a.m.)

½ to 1 cup of milk mixed with 2 to 4 tbsps of *dalia* (broken wheat) or oats

½ to 1 half-boiled egg

10-drops/½ tsp of Vidaylin-M drops/syrup

1 tsp of Ostocalcium/ Ossopan syrup

Midday (11 a.m.)

25 to 100 gm minced chicken/meat/beef with soup

Boiled vegetables, such as carrots, potatoes, cabbage

50 to 100 gm boiled rice

½ tsp of Vitapet/cod liver oil

Afternoon (4 p.m.)

Repeat 7.30 a.m. diet with only milk and porridge

Evening (9 p.m.)

Repeat 11 a.m. diet with only minced chicken/meat and rice.

Diet alternatives and suggestions

- Bread/rusks/chapatis can be given in place of rice.
- Farex/Cerelac can take the place of wheat *dalia*/oats porridge for a small puppy.

- Visyneral multivitamin drops can be used in place of Vidaylin-M drops.
- Kalzana/Macalvit syrup can be given in place of Ostocalcium/ Ossopan syrup.
- Half to one teaspoon of Bonisan Syrup can be given to puppies to treat minor digestive disorders.
- Milk and eggs can replace chicken or meat.
- Half to one teaspoon of Complan should be added to undiluted milk for weak puppies.
- Yeast powder/Promix-Y tablets should be given after the age of three months.
- Soyabean flour can be added to wheat flour in the ratio of 1:3 to make it more nourishing.
- Raw carrots can be fed after the age of three months.
- Home-made *paneer* (cottage cheese) can substitute meat if you want your dog to be a vegetarian.
- After the age of three months, young dogs can be fed thrice a day instead of four times.
- After the age of six months, feed your dog twice a day. Gradually increase the amount of food as he grows older.

Is it possible to rear a puppy on a totally vegetarian diet?

You can give your puppy vegetarian food, though it is very difficult to formulate a balanced vegetarian diet that meets the nutritional requirements of a growing dog. Dogs are carnivorous and love to eat a non-vegetarian diet, but if you can ensure that the puppy's diet contains adequate proteins, by giving eggs, milk and soyabeans, it is alright. Many nutritionally balanced, commercially prepared, ready-made dry vegetarian dog foods have been introduced in the Indian market, with which you can feed your dog. However, you must

discuss the diet schedule with your vet, to avoid any nutritional deficiency.

What factors affect the nutritional requirements of a puppy or dog?

The following factors affect a puppy's or dog's nutritional requirements:

- Disease often increases the requirement for certain nutrients such as vitamins, and decreases the dog's ability to process or digest other nutrients.
- Age affects protein and mineral requirements and energy needs.
- Activity levels change energy needs.
- Environmental changes such as extreme heat, cold, humidity or stress can affect nutritional requirements.
- Temperament affects energy needs, and a highly strung puppy or dog will need a high-energy diet.
- Pregnant and nursing female dogs need an increased amount of energy, proteins, vitamins and certain minerals.

Helpful Tips for Feeding and Caring for Your Puppy

- Initially follow the breeder's instructions and menu when feeding the new puppy, and make dietary changes gradually.
- Feed him milk with Farex, *dalia* (wheat gruel) and *suji* (semolina) initially.
- Puppies get stomach upsets/diarrhoea due to change in environment, but settle down in twenty-four hours. Seek veterinary help if the problem persists for longer than that.
- Give your puppy multivitamin drops (cod liver oil and Osto Calcium) regularly till he is nine months old.
- Include minced meat/chicken, boiled eggs, milk, and green vegetables, rice/bread/chapatis in the puppy's food.
- Do not feed him mutton/chicken/fish bones.

- Feed your puppy at fixed times every day.
- Give him four meals a day for three months, three meals a day between three to six months, and thereafter, feed your dog only twice a day.
- Provide him with enough fresh, clean, drinking water at all times.
- Avoid feeding the puppy savory and sweet food.
- Always give him fresh and lukewarm food.
- Minimize excitement and physical activity before, during, and for an hour after meals.
- If you want to feed your puppy commercial dog food, use one made by a reputed manufacturer and follow the instructions on the pack. The change over from fresh to dry commercial food should be gradual—over a period of seven to ten days. At first, mix the dry food with the fresh, and over a few days, increase the quantity of dry food and decrease that of fresh food.

House-training (Toilet-training)

By about five weeks of age most puppies urinate and defecate in a far corner of their whelping box; a result of the natural instinct to keep their bed clean. You can utilize this instinct by starting house-training, with the help of a dog crate or portable kennel, as soon as the puppy joins your household. The crate should be just big enough for him to stand up, turn around and stretch. If it is too large, it will give the puppy enough room to urinate and defecate away from his bed, so he will not feel the need to control his bladder or bowel movements. Therefore, by keeping him in the crate, you can teach him bowel and bladder control. However, do not leave a young puppy in the crate for more than four hours at a time, and never allow him to roam freely in the house, unsupervised. The idea of keeping a puppy in a crate or

portable kennel is to limit his freedom and establish a set routine or schedule, so that he can be taken out to a particular place at fixed intervals, and after every meal urinate or defecate. After taking the puppy to the designated area, give the command 'GO POTTY', and reward him by saying 'GOOD DOG' after he has urinated or defecated. By repeating this routine, he will understand that he has to go out to answer the call of nature. However, it is not easy to house-train a puppy, and there will be accidents; one should have patience and control one's temper always. Gentle but firm handling is required to train puppies.

How does one house-train a puppy?

House-training means training the puppy or dog to answer the call of nature outside the house. It is a very important aspect of puppy or dog management for which every dog owner should make an effort to find time. Dogs never soil or dirty their beds or sleeping areas. They usually select specific places inside or outside the house and use them again and again, especially to urinate. As a dog owner, you will have to decide where these places should be. Get your puppy used to a particular place. It is customary to train a puppy to use a newspaper in the house, and later on, the grass outside. Dog's stool has an unpleasant odour and can be a minor health hazard. You should immediately wash your hands after cleaning up. Normally puppies urinate

or defecate after eating, drinking, playing, or on waking up. Very young puppies urinate every couple of hours and more frequently during the winter months. Sniffing the ground is often the only sign exhibited when the puppy wants to urinate or defecate. Some puppies also run around frantically just before passing stool. Pick up the puppy immediately and put him on the paper or on the selected area. Keep a small piece of soiled newspaper, along with a fresh one, to encourage the puppy to use the paper again. After he has urinated, praise him (by stroking his head and neck gently, and calling his name). Do not scold the puppy if the floor is accidentally soiled, and never forcibly put the puppy's nose into the mess. Clean the area with a deodorant spray. Do not use ammonia disinfectant as it may remind the puppy of the smell of urine. An older puppy should be trained to go outside. The first thing in the morning should be to take the puppy outside for a short walk in the same general area every day and let him sniff around. Praise the puppy when he urinates and defecates. He should also be taken out after he is fed. Again at night, before going to sleep, take him for a short stroll. Soon it will become a habit with him, and he will bark and run to the door whenever he wants to urinate or defecate. With a little effort, you can also train your dog to use the bathroom in the house.

Are there any aids that help in house-training a puppy?

A puppy-trainer spray is available in the West. It encourages puppies to urinate or defecate in a particular place. Puppy-trainer sprays can be used on newspapers or outside the house.

Is there any particular aid that prevents puppies from urinating or defecating at a particular spot or carpet in the house?

A product called NO-GO is available in the USA. It is effective in preventing puppies from urinating on the same spot on the carpet

every time. There are also pads called piddle pads or puppy-training pads which contain a special scent that attracts puppies, and they use them wherever they are kept. These pads can be gradually moved from inside the house to outdoors and once they become familiar with the scent, they soon learn to go outside to urinate or defecate.

Is it true that all puppies have worms and some of these can be passed on to humans? How can one prevent this from happening?

Most puppies get worm infections from their mothers, either at the prenatal stage, or soon after birth through the mother's milk. Roundworms and tapeworms can be passed on by puppies to humans, especially to young children, and can create health problems. Therefore, puppies should be dewormed when they are four weeks old, and after that every month till they are six months old. Their stool should be removed and flushed in the toilet immediately, and the area cleaned. Children and adults should always wash their hands before eating food if they have handled puppies or dogs.

Why does the grass in the lawn get brown patches at those places where the dog urinates?

Dog urine is acidic, therefore it burns the grass, leaving a brown patch.

How long does it take to house-train a puppy?

With consistent effort, a set routine, and patience, it is possible to house-train a puppy in three to four weeks' time. Younger puppies take a little longer than older ones. Praise the puppy lavishly, saying 'GOOD BOY' when he uses the newspaper. If he urinates or defecates at other places, say 'NO' in a firm tone. When you take the puppy outdoors, do not leave him alone; stay close by and watch him carefully. After sniffing around he will do the needful. Call him by his name, praise and pat him, and then bring him inside.

How can I prevent my puppy from dirtying the carpet?

Puppies are stimulated to defecate or urinate by smelling carpets. So roll up all the carpets in your house till such time as the puppy is house-trained.

How often should I take my puppy out to answer the call of nature?

A five to six-week-old puppy should be taken out every two hours. In addition, he must be taken out immediately after every feed and the moment he starts sniffing around in the house. Take your puppy out soon after he wakes up in the morning, and also at night just before going to sleep. After he is three months old, he will need to be taken out four to five times during the day.

How many times does a puppy normally defecate and urinate?

At five to six weeks, puppies defecate four to five times a day. Normally, they do so in the morning and after every feed when they are taken out. They urinate more often in winter.

How much sleep does a puppy require during the day?

Like human babies, puppies sleep a lot; generally up to six or eight hours during the day. After feeding and playing a little, they go to sleep.

Is it normal for puppies to sometimes whine while asleep?

Puppies sometimes whine while asleep, as if they are dreaming. It is quite normal.

Young puppies are very destructive and they bite, chew socks, shoes, wooden furniture, and so forth. How does one prevent this?

All puppies love chewing and biting hard objects because of the teething stimulus. Some grown-up dogs also do this, especially when

nobody is watching them. Boredom and lack of proper exercise is often the main cause of destructive chewing in grown-up dogs. To prevent your puppy from chewing shoes, socks and furniture, give him a few rubber toys and rubber bones to play with and chew. At the same time, whenever you catch him gnawing at household furniture, shoes and other things, scold him, saying 'NO' firmly, and give his collar a shake. This will convey to him that what he is doing is wrong. Also try and keep the puppy away from furniture and shoes so that he cannot get at them. Exercising him and playing with him in your lawn or a park is an antidote to boredom. Remember that scolding him will be effective only if you do it when you catch him chewing something, so that he can correlate the reprimand with what he has done. It will not have any effect if it is done after a lapse of time. Never hit or slap your puppy while reprimanding him. The tone of your voice, or gently hitting him with a rolled newspaper on the back, will sufficiently convey your displeasure. Sometimes, this habit is caused by dietary deficiencies, which should be discussed with your vet.

Grooming and Bathing

Grooming is the key to canine health and hygiene. It involves brushing and combing the coat, and cleaning the eyes, ears and teeth. The dog is also checked for ticks, fleas or other ectoparasites. Grooming improves a dog's appearance and removes the dead hair and dirt from his coat. It also stimulates blood circulation, as a result of which the skin and coat remain healthy and clean. A glossy coat denotes that the dog is healthy, whereas a dry and coarse one, with hair being shed constantly, means that something is wrong with him. Normally, dogs shed hair twice a year (March/April and October/November), although some hair is shed throughout the year. A lot of hair is shed after whelping and following a serious sickness. Worm infestation can also be a cause of hair shedding. Long-haired dogs need more grooming than short-haired ones to keep them clean. Grooming also provides an opportunity for bonding between owner and dog. Puppies should be introduced to grooming at an early age so that they enjoy it when older. To make grooming interesting for your puppy or dog, reward him after it is over. Through this regular interaction and grooming, the dog will accept you as the leader and willingly accept his own subordinate position. Also, while grooming your pet, you will be able to identify any existing health problems. Dogs tend to get bored if grooming is prolonged, therefore do not take more than ten minutes to groom your dog.

A dog that is groomed every day needs a bath once in fifteen or thirty days, depending on weather conditions. Dogs should be bathed as infrequently as possible, as bathing removes the natural protective oil from their hair, making it brittle and dry. A dog's skin is rich in oil glands producing oily secretions; this keeps the skin supple and makes the coat glossy. It also makes the hair water resistant. Dogs should be bathed either when they smell or when their coats are sufficiently dirty. Bathe your dog with slightly warm water, using a mild dog shampoo or soap, and take care that soap water does not get into his eyes or ears. Rinse, ensuring that all the soap is removed, and then dry him with a towel. Never use carbolic soap for bathing dogs. Also, it is better to groom him before giving him a bath. During winter, bathe him on a sunny day, preferably before noon (11 a.m. to noon is ideal) and make sure he isn't exposed to a draught.

When should one start grooming a puppy, and what are the benefits?

Grooming is a very important aspect of dog care, and all puppies and dogs should be groomed at least once a day. Short-haired dogs such as Labradors or Boxers require lesser grooming than long-haired breeds such as the Spitz or Cocker Spaniels. Start grooming your puppy from day one. Begin with a short session, just moving the brush and comb superficially over his body. Keep talking to him cheerfully as you are doing this, and then give him a treat, reward or praise him. You may need someone to hold the puppy initially when you groom him. Soon he will start enjoying it and then you can brush him more vigorously.

What are the essential items in a grooming kit?

A good brush and comb, preferably made of steel, are required for grooming. Some additional items, such as a wire brush, a rubber brush, a nail clipper, a pair of scissors, forceps, cotton wool, chamois cloth, ear buds and an antiseptic solution, should also be available.

Do dogs shed more hair during certain times of the year?

Dogs that stay outdoors shed hair twice a year, while those kept indoors shed it all the time. However, all dogs shed their winter coat in March/April.

What is the sequence of grooming?

The sequence of grooming for short-haired puppies or dogs is as follows:

- First use the rubber brush, brushing against the direction of the hair, so as to loosen dead hair and surface dirt.
- Next use the bristle brush to remove the dead hair, from head to tail. While grooming your dog, check for ticks or fleas or any other skin disorder. Clean the tail with a fine comb.

- Lastly, rub the coat with chamois cloth or your hands to make it shine, and clean the ears, eyes and anal area with cotton wool and a mild antiseptic solution.

The grooming sequence for long-haired dogs is as follows:

- Remove tangled hair or knots using a wire (slicker) brush.
- Brush the coat with a pin brush.
- Comb the hair throughout the body and legs using a wide-toothed comb.
- Trim extra long hair around the feet and hocks, which can lodge foreign bodies, dirt, and so on.
- Clean the eyes, ears and paws.

When should one start bathing a puppy and how often should he be bathed?

Normally, regular and proper grooming keeps a puppy's coat healthy and clean. You can, however, start bathing him when he is about four months old. During summer bathe him every fifteen or twenty days; and in winter, once a month on a clear, sunny day (around midday) with warm water. Do not bathe your puppy on a cold, wet day.

What is the sequence to be followed while bathing a puppy or dog?

The sequence given below should be followed while bathing a puppy or dog:

- Groom him properly before bathing him.
- Plug his ears with cotton wool.
- Make him stand in a plastic bathtub, or take him outdoors.
- Holding the puppy or dog by his collar, pour tepid water on his body. You may need someone to hold him when you bathe him first.
- Rub shampoo or dog soap into his wet coat to loosen dirt and dead hair.

- Shampoo his head, taking care not to get soap into his eyes or mouth.
- Wash the body thoroughly, and then the head, ensuring that all the shampoo or soap has been removed. The dog will shake his body to remove excess water as soon as you have finished bathing him.
- Squeeze out any remaining water with your hands and then wipe him with a clean towel.
- Remove the earplugs and dry the inside of the ears.
- A hair dryer can be used to dry the coat of long-haired dogs. Set it on the warm (not hot) setting.
- Finally brush the coat with a wire brush.
- Keep the dog on a leash or chained, or put him in his kennel to prevent him from rolling on the ground after his bath.

How do I clean my dog's eyes and ears?

You should clean your dog's eyes and ears after grooming him every day. Clean the eyes with cotton wool moistened with water, gently removing any discharge sticking under the eyes. Similarly, the inside of your dog's ear flap should be cleaned by holding it open with one hand and cleaning it with moistened cotton wool, use fresh cotton wool; for each ear. Never probe the inner ear cavity deeply, as it can injure your dog's ears. Dogs with long, pendulous ears, such as Cocker Spaniels or Basset Hounds, need regular ear-cleaning. Consult your vet if you find any unusual discharge from your puppy or dog's eyes or ears.

Basic Obedience Training and Exercise for Puppies

Start training your puppy from the very first day you bring him home. A well-trained dog is a pleasure to own, but you will have to behave like a leader in order to train your puppy. Puppies follow their mother or leader in the wild, like wolves. If you are not in command, they will take advantage of the situation and misbehave. Therefore, it is very important to discipline and train your puppy from an early age. Puppies and dogs are sociable animals. Therefore being in contact with people and other dogs is stimulating for them. Keeping a puppy isolated for long periods is undesirable, as he will behave in a wild manner and get overexcited when he meets you after a long period of separation. In such an excited state he will not be amenable to discipline.

The first thing you should do is name your puppy. Always address him by this name, so that he associates it with himself and responds when called by it. After he has learnt his name, he should be taught the meaning of the word NO. It is a reprimand and should only be used when you catch him doing something wrong. A sharp 'NO' will stop him in his tracks, if accompanied by an angry look and an index finger raised in a forbidding manner. The nature of the training should be in accordance with the age of the puppy. In six to eight weeks he should have learned to sleep in his own bed, respond to his name, and be reasonably house-trained.

At about three or four months the puppy should gradually be introduced to basic words of command, such as 'SIT', 'DOWN', 'STAY',

'COME', 'GO' and 'OUT'. Encouragement and praise, saying 'GOOD DOG', and petting him on his chest, make a dog much more responsive to training. He can also be given some titbits as a reward for good behaviour and his positive response to the training. Never punish your puppy or dog by hitting him, as this will only scare him and he will start avoiding you. The best way of training your dog is by combining firmr.ess with kindness. Handle him gently. Dogs learn by hearing the same command repeated over and over again, so you have to be very patient and kind while training them. Basic obedience training is necessary for every dog so that he can become a good companion and a responsible member of the family.

WALKING AT HEEL

Daily exercise is essential to keep a puppy or dog in good health. The breed and size dictate the amount of exercise needed. Dogs benefit most from regular exercise everyday rather than long exercise periods on weekends, and it is important to stick to a routine when exercising them. Young dogs, especially large breeds, should be exercised cautiously to prevent damage to their joints. They should never be allowed to run freely without a leash until they are fully trained.

When should a puppy start wearing a collar and leash?

A puppy should be fitted with a neck collar as soon he comes to the house. A leash can be used during brief training sessions from the age of ten to twelve weeks.

Should one use a choke collar?

For puppies of larger breeds, choke collars

COME

are helpful to teach them to walk at heel if they tend to pull ahead or refuse to walk. The collar tightens around their necks, causing discomfort, and forces them to walk at heel. However, there is the risk of injury if the collar is not fitted properly.

When should one begin to train a puppy?

Basic training can begin with house-training, soon after the new puppy comes to the house. Encourage him to sit before you place his food in front of him. Sitting is a natural posture for dogs and with the help of gentle pressure exerted on the hindquarters the puppy will sit. Always call him by his name so that he learns it quickly. Once he learns his name, the puppy's response to training will be much faster.

STAY

How long should a training session last?

Since puppies have short concentration spans, formal training sessions should not be more then ten minutes in duration. There should not be any distractions for them in the place selected for training. Make training sessions interesting for your puppy by encouraging him all the time, and give him titbits when he reacts positively.

How often should the training session be repeated?

Repeat the training session several times a day for short periods, so that the puppy does not get

SIT

bored. Mornings and evenings are best suited for training sessions; the progress made is directly proportional to the time devoted to it.

What are the essential commands for basic training?

The essential commands are: 'SIT', 'DOWN', 'STAY', 'COME', 'NO' and 'HEEL'. You should start with 'SIT' and 'HEEL'. Other commands can follow gradually.

How do I teach my puppy to walk in a straight line on my left at heel position?

With your puppy on a leash, take the help of a wall or a fence, and keep him sandwiched between you and the wall or fence, so that he cannot pull away at an angle. Keep walking with him on your left, just behind you. Go on repeating the word HEEL whenever he tries to pull ahead or lags behind. Do not forget to get his attention by calling him by his name first, and then saying 'HEEL'. He will soon learn to walk in a straight line.

Should I allow my puppy to socialize with other dogs?

Until your puppy has been given his basic immunization shots, it is not advisable to let him socialize with other puppies or dogs. When he is twelve to fourteen weeks old, allow him to interact with other healthy puppies or dogs that have been immunized. This will help him to communicate and play with other puppies or dogs, and will make him less nervous and more accommodating in nature.

How many times a day should I take my puppy out for walks?

Take him out for a walk at least once a day, though twice is preferable. It is better to take your puppy on different routes to allow him to learn more about your neighbourhood and environment. If you live in a house with a large compound, he will manage to get enough exercise by running around and playing.

How can I stop my puppy from chewing my hand?

A puppy instinctively uses its mouth to explore the texture of objects, including a person's hand. He is unlikely to bite, but sometimes, when excited, his sharp teeth can puncture the skin. Do not encourage him to play with your hand as this may develop into a bad habit with serious consequences as the puppy grows older. When he starts chewing your hand, you should withdraw it immediately and scold him with a sharp 'NO'. This will give him a corrective message. Give him a puppy chew to satisfy his biting instinct.

How do I teach my puppy to drop a ball while playing?

The puppy must be taught the command 'DROP' at an early age, to prevent him from becoming over possessive and biting you when you try to take an object from his mouth. First call his name to draw his attention, then open his mouth by pulling up his upper jaw with your left hand and the lower jaw with your right one, and at the same time firmly say 'DROP'. When the mouth is forcibly opened, the ball will fall out. This should be repeated several times, as it is an important lesson, and the puppy must learn to drop anything in his mouth on hearing the command 'DROP'.

How can I train my puppy not to damage furniture or chew things?

A puppy (up to the age of six months) loves to chew anything, as he is teething. He should not be left free to roam around the house. It is better to keep him confined in a room or kennel. Do, however, give him some dog chews to gnaw at. Exercise the puppy adequately and do not allow him to get bored. Corrective supervision, by keeping chewable objects out of his reach, and checking him with a stern 'NO' when caught chewing, will help.

How can I prevent my puppy from climbing up on a sofa or bed?

Do not allow the puppy to sit on a sofa or bed. From the start, he should be provided with a separate bed of his own, and children should not be allowed to carry him to a bed or sofa. A puppy that has not been allowed to do so will not normally try to jump on one. However, if he does, sternly order him to 'GET DOWN' and take him to his bed.

How can I teach my puppy to sit?

Do this when you are going to feed the puppy. Hold the food bowl over his head, so as to draw his attention to it. To keep his eyes on the bowl, the puppy will sit down. Simultaneously, you should say 'SIT', and reward him with his meal. By repeating this several times, even a very young puppy will learn to sit without much difficulty.

How do I teach my puppy to lie down?

After the puppy has learnt to sit, he should be taught to lie down. When he is sitting, sit down by his side and say 'DOWN', and at the same time pat the ground in front of him. He may ignore the command, but you should gently pull his front legs forward and press down his body, and saying 'DOWN', make him lie down.

How can I teach my puppy the command 'STAY'?

The aim of teaching the command 'STAY' is to train the puppy to remain in the same position he was in when the command was given. After you bring him to the DOWN position, sit in front of him and give the command 'STAY'. When he moves or changes his position, persuade him to stay in the DOWN position by repeating the word STAY. After hearing it repeated several times, and being encouraged to remain in the same position he was in when the command was given, he will learn the command.

How should I teach my puppy to come to me when I call him?

The puppy must first know his name; only then will he respond to it. He may not obey if he is not on a leash, or if there are distractions such as strong scents in the area. To teach him to come to you when called while on a leash, lightly pull or jerk the leash, and at the same time call him by his name. Then say 'COME' gently, several times. You should be patient and make much of the puppy when he comes to you, so as to reinforce the bond between you and him.

How do I teach the command 'OUT' to my puppy?

This command is taught to the puppy so that he leaves the room and goes to his own room or bed when there are guests who do not like dogs or are afraid of them. To teach this command keep the puppy on a long leash. There should be another person holding the other end of the leash outside the room near his bed. Call the puppy by his name and say 'OUT', and at the same time gesture with your right index finger, indicating that he should leave the room. Simultaneously, the other person should pull the leash gently to make the dog go to his own bed. By repeating this process several times, the puppy will learn to go OUT when ordered to do so.

How do I teach the command 'NO' to my puppy?

The command 'NO' is used as a rebuke or reprimand. Therefore it should be said in a sharp tone, to differentiate it from other words of command or praise. To reinforce this command, either hit the ground while saying it, or jerk the leash. After this is repeated several times, the puppy will understand that NO is a reprimand to check an undesirable activity. You must be consistent in the manner you give commands to your puppy, as dogs respond to the tone of voice and the hand signs associated with it. They do not understand language,

but mentally correlate the sound or tone of particular words indicating the actions they are required to perform. They understand single-syllable words such as NO and SIT better than long verbal commands.

How do I teach my puppy to walk at heel?

Walking at heel means that the puppy walks correctly on your left side with his right shoulder in line with your left knee. This position is safe for the dog and the owner can easily control him. The puppy should be taught this command after he is three months old, on completion of his vaccination schedule, and after having learnt to walk in a straight line. In order to teach this command, take him out on a leash with a neck collar to a quiet place or a park where there is minimum disturbance or distraction. Start walking, holding the leash in your right hand, and keeping the puppy on your left side. Call him by his name to draw his attention, and then give the command 'HEEL'; at the same time give a slight jerk to the leash with your left hand to bring him in line with your left knee. If he pulls forward, gently jerk him back; if he lags behind or pulls in an outward direction, gently pull him forward to bring him to the correct position. Jerking or pulling at the leash and the command 'HEEL' should be simultaneous, so that the puppy correlates the sound of the word HEEL with his walking at the correct heel position. After practising for a few days, he will learn to do this correctly. Lavish him with praise when he does so. However, the duration of each lesson should not be more than ten to fifteen minutes.

How should I offer a treat to my puppy as a reward for his having obeyed a command?

Giving food or titbits to a puppy, such as a small piece of cheese, liver

or meat, or a biscuit, as a reward for a command correctly executed is an excellent training aid. The treat should be kept hidden between the thumb and index finger of the left hand, with the palm closed. The puppy should be rewarded more frequently during the initial training period. With time, food treats can be given less frequently; they can be substituted with verbal and physical (touch) praise saying, 'GOOD DOG', and petting or stroking him on the chest or head. However, verbal praise is never as effective as food or touch rewards.

Is it safe to take my puppy to play and exercise in a public park?

A puppy should be taken to a public place only after he has been given the complete course of immunization shots. The first of these is given when he is six to seven weeks old and is repeated at four-week intervals. Therefore, do not take your puppy to public parks before he is four months old. You can, however, let him out in your own garden or lawn, provided it is enclosed and is not accessible to stray dogs. This will help in house-training him.

Should I take my puppy for a walk on a leash with a collar or a harness?

A well-fitting harness with adjustable straps should be used for puppies or dogs of smaller breeds. It exerts less stress on the neck area. A leash and collar are suitable for puppies of bigger breeds, as they can withstand more pressure on the vertebral column and the trachea, compared to smaller dogs.

How far should I take my puppy for his daily walk?

Two or three short walks are better than one long walk. Start with a one-kilometre walk, and gradually increase it to three to five kilometres, depending on the size of the dog.

What precautions should I take while exercising my dog in summer?

Puppies and dogs do not enjoy walking in hot weather, as they do not have enough sweat glands to cope with the heat. They do not perspire as efficiently as human beings (as their sweat glands are confined only to a small area between their toes), and depend on panting and evaporation from their nasal cavities to cool their bodies. Puppies and dogs with long, thick coats have more problems during hot weather. Therefore be very careful while exercising your dog in summer.

What precautions should I take when exercising my dog during winter?

Short-haired puppies or dogs need to be protected from cold and damp weather in winter. They should wear warm coats when they are taken for walks. It is advisable to take them to a veterinary clinic and get them a coat that fits properly.

Can I take my dog for a walk without a leash?

Dogs should never be taken out without a leash, as they are prone to road accidents. They should not be allowed to run freely on public roads either, even if they are well trained. Allow your dog to play freely in a confined area, and to run around and explore, as this will give him a feeling of freedom. Get an extendable leash for him, it will give him some freedom, and at the same time you will be able to control him.

Helpful Tips for Training and Exercise

- House-train the puppy by placing newspapers on the floor.
- Reward him promptly after he complies with a command.
- Reprimand him immediately after every act of disobedience.
- Keep training periods short, interspersed with play intervals.

- Do not lose your temper while training your dog.
- Teach him only one thing at a time.
- Too many masters or trainers will confuse the dog. There should be only one person in command.
- While training a dog, fixed words should be used as verbal commands, in the same tone and manner.
- Always keep your dog on a leash.
- Finish training your dog on a successful note.
- Never hit your dog, just say 'BAD BOY' to point out his mistakes.
- Do not exercise your puppy or dog strenuously until he is nine months old.
- Make time for frequent play sessions with your puppy.
- Do not allow your puppy to socialize with stray or strange dogs or take him to public places until his full course of vaccination is complete (at about sixteen weeks).
- Allow the puppy to socialize with selected people and vaccinated dogs. It is beneficial for him.

Teething and Preventive Health Care

Puppies are toothless when they are born. At four to six weeks of age their milk teeth erupt (fourteen in the upper jaw and fourteen in the lower jaw). These fall out when they are between four to five months old, and are replaced by permanent teeth at six months. All permanent teeth (forty-two in number) are out between the ages of nine to twelve months. The front incisors (six in each jaw) are comparatively small and are used for scraping the food; the canines (two in each jaw) are the longest teeth, which are used for biting and tearing, and the pre-molars and molars (twenty-six in number) crush and cut the

food into small pieces. There can be wide variation in the wear and tear of permanent teeth in a dog, so it is not possible to assess the age of a dog by examining his teeth.

Why do some dogs have bad breath and how can one prevent this?

Bad breath is a sign of gum disease. Most dogs develop this problem by the time they are four or five years old. Regular cleaning of the teeth, along with professional scaling by a vet, can prevent bad breath and gum disease.

Some puppies do not shed their milk canines and the permanent canines erupt behind them. What should one do if this happens?

This problem is common in puppies when they are about six months old. A vet should extract the milk teeth in order to make place for the permanent set.

Why do smaller breeds suffer more from dental problems?

The teeth of smaller breeds are more closely packed together, so they need more attention than larger breeds.

Are some breeds more prone to dental problems?

Some breeds, such as Boxers and Bull Terriers, are more likely to suffer from proliferative gum disease.

Do chewing bones or stones damage the teeth of dogs?

Yes, it does, and it also causes infection. Dogs should not be encouraged to chew bones or stones.

Preventive Health Care

Prevention is always better than cure, and preventive health care is a wise investment because it costs substantially less than treatment. It can increase the quality and length of your pet's life and ensure greater vitality and fewer health problems.

What vaccines do puppies need and at what age?

Puppies are especially susceptible to several bacterial and viral diseases. The passive immunity inherited from their mother declines after they are ten to twelve weeks old. Therefore, it is essential that they are immunized actively through the administration of prophylactic vaccines to give them protection against these diseases. Their vaccination programme starts at the age of six weeks, when they get their first immunization shot for distemper, hepatitis (adenovirus), parvovirus, corona virus and leptospirosis. Four weeks later, they are given a booster, followed by another booster shot when they are fourteen weeks old. After this, annual booster shots have to be administered to adult dogs. The first immunization shot against rabies is given to puppies at the age of three months, followed by a booster after six months, and thereafter, annual booster shots are administered. Annual booster shots are indispensable for the maintenance of a proper level of immunity against contagious or infectious diseases. When puppies are vaccinated, the vaccine induces a response in the body cells which produces antibodies to a specific disease. Should they come into contact with the disease at a later date, the antibodies neutralize the bacteria or virus causing the disease and prevent the infection from taking hold. Puppies vary in their capacity to respond to vaccinations; there are no hundred per cent guarantees that

they are fully protected against a specific disease. However, almost ninety per cent are protected once they have time to develop antibodies, provided they receive booster vaccinations at the recommended time.

Deworming

What is the schedule for deworming puppies to keep them worm-free?

Almost all puppies inherit worms from their mothers. The breeder normally deworms them at the age of four weeks. Another de worming, a week before the vaccination against distemper, hepatitis, parvovirus, corona virus and leptospirosis, follows this. Puppies are dewormed every month after that with a broad-spectrum deworming agent till they are six months old. Thereafter, deworming is done on a quarterly basis. Your vet will advise you regarding the frequency of deworming required for your pet. It is also advisable for members of your family, especially children who can get a worm infection from the puppy, to be regularly dewormed. For this you must consult your physician.

Helpful Tips for Teething and Health Care

- Providing chewable toys for your puppy will prevent him from chewing objects in the house.
- Excessive chewing is most likely to occur first when the puppy is three months old, and then between six to twelve months when the permanent teeth erupt.
- Vaccinations help in preventing many devastating and often fatal infectious diseases by stimulating the dog's immune system.

- Always adhere to your puppy's vaccination schedule.
- Booster shots are essential for reinforcing protective immunity.
- Regular deworming of puppies, starting from the age of three to four weeks, is imperative for controlling intestinal worms.
- Regular veterinary check-ups are necessary for all puppies.

2

the adult dog

A dog is considered an adult when he is ten months old, soon after attaining his full height. The habits and training acquired by him as a puppy remain with him when he attains maturity. It is difficult to correct the bad habits of an adult dog, so it is important that a puppy is trained properly.

CARE AND MANAGEMENT OF AN ADULT DOG

An adult dog, like a puppy, also has to be groomed, fed and housed properly. The procedure for grooming a puppy and an adult dog is the same. You should groom your dog at least once a day. An adult dog can be fed only once daily, but feeding him twice a day is better. He must have his own bed to sleep in, especially at night. Like a puppy, an adult dog should not be encouraged to sit on chairs, sofas or beds. Water should always be available in a bowl which is cleaned daily. An adult dog needs to be exercised every day by walking him for at least thirty minutes; large breeds should also be made to run. The basic obedience training imparted should be continued, so that he does not forget the commands learnt as a puppy. Clean your dog's eyes and ears daily (the ears need the professional attention of a vet at monthly intervals), examine the teeth, and remove tartar deposits with wet gauze. Periodic scaling of the teeth by a vet is strongly recommended. The nails of some adult dogs (especially those that do not get adequate exercise) need periodic clipping, and their feet have to be checked for foreign bodies while they are being groomed. Ensure that your dog gets its annual booster shots for rabies, distemper, hepatitis, parvovirus, corona virus and leptospirosis.

Checklist for the Care of Adult Dogs

- Groom your dog for at least ten minutes every day.
- Always check for ticks, fleas and other ectoparasites while grooming him.
- Clean his eyes and ears daily, removing the wax from the ears with wet cotton wool.
- Do not bathe your dog too often (once a month is enough) and ensure that he does not catch a chill.
- Make sure that clean water is always available in the water bowl for him.
- Do not feed your adult dog more than twice a day.
- Follow a daily routine for exercise, grooming and feeding.
- Do not feed table scraps to your dog.
- Do not feed him sweets, deep-fried and ice-cold food, hard-boiled eggs, pork.
- Never give chicken, fish or mutton bones to your dog.
- Do not overfeed your dog.
- Ensure that he walks for at least thirty minutes every day.
- Keep reinforcing his basic training, and expose him to advanced training when his brain is fully developed.
- Deworm your adult dog every three months.
- Protect him from rabies, distemper, hepatitis, parvovirus, corona virus and leptospirosis with yearly booster shots.
- Get your dog's teeth examined every six months, and have them scaled and cleaned when needed.
- Immediately consult your vet regarding any health problems your dog may have.
- Take your dog to the vet for regular check-ups; at least once a year. This is essential for the early detection of ailments.

Breeding, Pregnancy, Pre-natal Care and Whelping

Female dogs usually attain sexual maturity at the age of seven to nine months. However, females of larger breeds may take longer and become sexually mature at twelve to fifteen months of age, which is when they get their first oestrous cycle (season). Males then start sniffing them and marking their territory by urinating around the area. Dogs should be bred after they are two years old. By then female dogs would have had at least two seasons.

With the large number of surplus dogs in India, only healthy, pedigreed and very good specimens of a breed should be bred, so that the puppies can go to good homes. The oestrous cycle (season) of female dogs lasts for twenty-one days, and two matings should be carried out on the eleventh and thirteenth days. The gestation period of a female dog varies from sixty to sixty-five days (average sixty-three days). Generally, she looks after herself during whelping and no assistance is required. The mother cleans the puppies as soon as they are born and cuts the umbilical cords. The puppies start suckling as soon as they are born; they open their eyes after twelve days, and are weaned at the age of six to eight weeks, when they are ready to go to new homes.

Rearing a litter of puppies is a delightful experience, though it entails hard work and care. Therefore, one should plan the breeding well in advance.

What are the first signs of the oestrous cycle in a female dog?

The first thing one sees is a few drops of blood or spotting. Further examination reveals that the vulva is swollen and there is a bloody discharge from it. The onset of the oestrous cycle is a sign that the female dog has attained sexual maturity and can reproduce. The bleeding continues for nine to ten days, but the swelling of the genitalia persists for almost three weeks. A female dog will normally permit mating after the ninth day of her season, which invariably results in pregnancy.

How does a male dog exhibit signs of sexual maturity?

On attaining sexual maturity, a male dog becomes more aggressive towards other male dogs and starts scenting female dogs in heat (season). He tends to wander when he catches the scent of oestrous. He also begins marking his territory by sprinkling his urine.

What is the best time for a female dog in oestrous to mate?

Although the oestrous cycle of a female dog lasts for nearly twenty-one days, the best days for mating are the eleventh and thirteenth days or the twelfth and fourteenth days of the oestrous cycle. The first day one notices the spotting is taken as day one of the cycle.

What precautions should one take for a female dog in season?

Since a female dog in season attracts male dogs, take her out on a leash with a long stick to scare away male dogs. Never let her roam freely or she may mate in front of you, ignoring your commands. This can result in unwanted puppies.

Is it true that a female dog should have at least one litter in her lifetime in order to improve her temperament?

There is no scientific evidence that demonstrates this.

What should one keep in mind when choosing a stud dog?

If your female dog is registered with the Kennel Club, look for a registered, young, healthy and experienced stud dog who has sired a litter before. The dogs should be mated on the premises of the owner of the stud dog.

During mating how does the tie' between a female dog and a stud dog take place?

At the back of the penis of a male dog there is a gland called the bulbo-urethral gland, which swells during copulation. As a result, it gets stuck in the female genitalia, causing a tie' with the female and male dogs standing, facing opposite directions. They should not be disturbed during this tie', which normally lasts for ten to fifteen minutes.

Should a male dog with only one testicle be mated?

It is not advisable to mate a female dog with a male dog with only one testicle. The terms for this condition is monorchid, and mating may not be successful. It is transmitted genetically and is therefore hereditary.

If a male dog has only one testicle in its scrotum, is it a cause for concern?

Normally both the testicles descend into the scrotum shortly after birth. In some dogs one testicle is retained in the abdomen. This can become cancerous and should be removed. The normal testicle should also be removed, as otherwise, if bred, the dog can pass on this condition to his offspring.

What are the breeding terms normally decided upon with the owner of the stud dog?

The stud dog's owner charges a stud fee, which is either refunded if the female dog does not conceive, or another mating during the next season is provided free of cost. Sometimes the stud dog's owner prefers to take the pick of the litter instead of the stud fee. The terms should be clearly agreed upon before the mating.

Can a dog contract sexually-transmitted diseases (STD) as a result of mating?

Dogs can contract several sexually-transmitted diseases such as canine herpes virus, brucellosis and canine venereal tumours during mating. These generally manifest themselves in and around the genitalia and in the mouth. Therefore, a veterinary examination of the stud dog is necessary before the mating.

Do female dogs have menopause like human females?

Female dogs do not have menopause and keep having their season even after they are ten years old. However, the periodicity of the season decreases.

Checklist for Breeding

- Choose a registered, young, healthy and experienced stud dog for the mating.
- Get the female dog and stud dog examined by your vet before mating them. This will ensure they are healthy, immunized and dewormed, and free from any sexually transmitted and heritable diseases.
- Introduce the female dog to the stud dog two or three days before the mating.
- The mating should be on the stud owner's premises.
- Have two matings, two days apart, on the eleventh and thirteenth days of the season.
- Reassure and comfort the female dog during the mating and ensure that the tie' lasts for ten minutes.
- Protect her from other male dogs till her season is over.
- When she is in season, ensure that she is always on a leash when you take her out.

Can a female dog have a litter sired by two or more dogs?

Two or more dogs can mate a female dog in one season. This often happens with stray female dogs Therefore, isolate your already mated female dog from male dogs till her season is over.

Pre-natal Care

How long, after mating, will it take for a vet to confirm her pregnancy?

Take her to the vet for a check-up four to five weeks after the mating. However, the first visible signs of pregnancy are observed after about thirty-five days of mating, when the nipples become prominent and the abdomen gets enlarged.

Why does a female dog sometimes not conceive after a planned mating? How can this be corrected/treated?

Either the male or the female dog could be responsible for her failure to conceive. The causes can be female genital-tract infections, herpes, brucellosis or canine venereal tumours. Get your dog examined and treated by a vet for any infection she may have. Also change the stud dog and use a proven sire in her next season.

When will the female dog come into season again if she does not conceive during the mating?

Female dogs generally have two seasons a year, but there are exceptions to the rule, and some have only one season. The time period between the two seasons also varies, ranging from two months to ten months.

What is a false or pseudo-pregnancy in a female dog?

Many female dogs that have not been mated show signs of pregnancy almost two months after their last season. Their mammary glands swell up and their breasts fill up with milk. Their temperament changes, and they become snappy, seeking dark corners in the house. Some take to nursing toys or socks as though puppies. This confuses their owners. However, this is purely a psychological condition, caused by a hormone known as progesterone, which stimulates the production of milk. This condition disappears after some time, provided the female dogs are taken out for long walks and are not allowed to hide in the house. Some female dogs may need hormonal treatment for this condition. It is advisable to get them spayed after the false pregnancy has subsided, as this condition can lead to metritis or pyometra (infection of the uterus), and is likely to recur. However, if you want your dog to have a litter first, then let her be bred as soon as possible.

What precautions should I take to ensure a smooth pregnancy and a healthy litter if my dog is found to be pregnant at the third-week check-up by the vet?

Follow the vet's advice. Increase her diet gradually by ten to twenty per cent after the fifth week of pregnancy, and start feeding her three times a day. Regular walking and grooming is also necessary. Avoid overfeeding her, especially during the first four weeks of pregnancy. She needs a balanced diet with additional proteins, calcium, phosphorous and multi-vitamins during the last five weeks. During the last two weeks, take her for short walks instead of a long one, and do not let her jump or run up and down the stairs. Feed her more often, and take her out for stool more often too.

What are the external signs of pregnancy in a female dog?

The abdomen of a pregnant dog starts getting larger after the fifth week of mating, and her teats start developing gradually. She sleeps and relaxes more than normal, and does not show much enthusiasm for walks.

Whelping (the birth process)

What preparations should be made for whelping?

ASSISTING WHELPING

Get a whelping box made, as shown in the drawing. Place it in a quiet corner of the house at least a week before the whelping, and let your dog start using it. Provide bedding in the box by using an old clean towel covered with newspaper. The whelping box prevents the newborn puppies from being accidentally crushed by the mother, or from wandering off. If your dog is long-haired, clip the excess matted hair around the vulva and clean the mammary glands gently with boiled, wet cotton wool. Inform your vet in advance about the expected date of whelping (sixty-three-day gestat period), and request him to make a house call, if req

PUP ENCASED IN FOETAL SAC

MOTHER LICKING THE NEWLY BORN

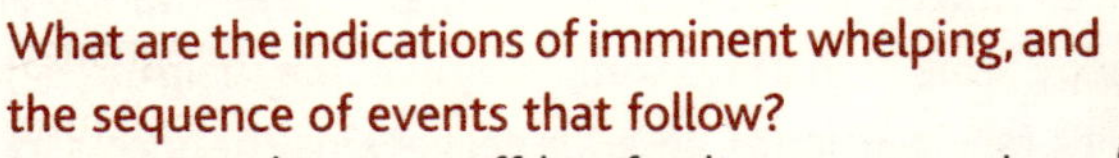

What are the indications of imminent whelping, and the sequence of events that follow?

A pregnant dog goes off her feed one or two days before whelping, becomes restless, and wants to stay in her whelping box. Her body temperature drops to almost 99.5 F; the vulva becomes enlarged, and the pelvic ligaments loose. She pants and sometimes shivers as the contractions start. At this stage, she may want to hide under a bed. She should be taken to her whelping box. This is the start

WHELPING BOX

of labour, and the water bag soon bursts, emitting fluid. The abdominal contractions become stronger and the dog circles round or lies down for the delivery. She keeps licking her vulva, and soon the puppy emerges, usually head first, encased in the amniotic sac. The mother breaks the sac by licking vigorously and the umbilical cord is cut as the puppy is delivered. She keeps licking her puppy vigorously. This stimulates the puppy and enables him to breathe. It also stimulates the puppy's urinary and faecal reflexes. The mother licks and clears away mucous from the mouth and nose of the puppy. The placenta is passed out ten to fifteen minutes after the birth of the puppy, and is normally eaten by the dog. After the first puppy is born, the mother rests for a while with the newborn puppy and prepares to deliver the remaining puppies. Normally they are born at half-hourly intervals.

When should one ask for the professional help of a vet?

The professional services of a vet are required if contractions do not start within two hours of the bursting of the water bag, or if the puppy does not emerge within fifteen minutes after the contractions begin. Non-productive contractions may be due to a breech presentation or an over-large puppy. Professional intervention by a vet may help the dog deliver her puppies, failing which a Caesarian delivery may be necessary.

How can I help my dog complete her whelping as quickly as possible?

A whelping dog tends to tire due to the contractions and the demanding task of cleaning and drying her puppies. Give her a cup of warm milk mixed with the yolk of an egg, or chicken soup, after each birth.

Are some breeds more prone to whelping problems?

Breeds such as Boxers, Bulldogs, Bull Mastiffs and Bull Terriers are more likely to have a difficult whelping, due to their large heads getting stuck in the birth canal. These breeds often need

veterinary help during whelping, especially those dogs whelping for the first time.

How do I know whether my dog has delivered all her puppies?

Generally, after delivering the last puppy and expelling the placenta, the mother dog stops panting, and settles down to feed her puppies. She may sometimes deliver her last puppy even twenty-four hours after the start of whelping. On the other hand, a dog that has not been able to deliver all her puppies will show signs of restlessness and sickness, such as fever, vomiting, complete loss of appetite, and will appear dull and depressed. Get her examined by the vet, who, after palpation of the abdomen, will be able to tell if there is still a puppy in the uterus. An X-ray of the abdomen may be required to confirm his diagnosis.

Sometimes there is a dirty and foul-smelling discharge emitted from the vagina of a recently whelped dog. What causes this and what should one do about it?

All whelping dogs shed some blood-tinged discharge for a few days after whelping. This is normal and is due to the involution of the uterus. However, if the discharge is more foul-smelling than normal and the dog is dull and depressed, it is an indication either of retention of the placenta or infection in the uterus. This can have serious consequences and calls for immediate veterinary attention.

Sometimes, after delivering her puppy, an inexperienced mother does not know what to do, and the puppy remains encased in the foetal sac. What should one do if this happens?

Immediately cut open the sac with a pair of sterilized scissors, or tear it open with clean fingers. Open the mouth of the puppy to enable him to start breathing, and rub him dry with a soft towel. If the mother has not cut the umbilical cord, tie it with a silk thread about four centimetres from the puppy's body, and then cut it below the knot. Apply Betadine liquid on the umbilical stump every day for the next three days.

Post-natal Care

The mother dog takes care of the newborn puppies, and for the first three weeks of their lives, they are totally dependent on her for food and security. However, one should ensure that they are kept warm and not exposed to a draught. Extreme changes in room temperature can have serious consequences, and many puppies catch a chill and die in winter if the room temperature is too low (below 70° F). The mother dog should be fed regular and nutritious meals so that she produces sufficient milk for her puppies. If she has an extra-large litter, top-feeding the puppies with a special canine milk formula may be necessary. After they are three weeks old, puppies require food supplements such as Farex with milk, in addition to their mother's milk. This helps in weaning them and also reduces the strain on the mother. At four weeks, puppies should be introduced to meat or chicken soup, boiled egg, wheat porridge, boiled rice and other milky cereals. The quantity of food given to them should be increased gradually, and when they are five to six weeks old the puppies will be ready to be weaned and leave for their new homes.

What should I feed my dog who has recently whelped so that she produces adequate milk for her puppies?

A dog that has recently whelped has a voracious appetite and needs special care in feeding so that she can produce adequate milk. Feed her three to four times a day. One meal should be milk and broken wheat (*dalia*) porridge with a boiled egg. Also give her protein-rich

food (eggs, boiled chicken or mutton without bones), minerals such as calcium and phosphorous, and vitamins. Increase the quantity of milk given to her as the puppies grow bigger. As a thumb rule, give her fifty per cent more than her usual intake of food in the first week after whelping, and double the amount at the start of the second week. By the time the puppies are three weeks old, the mother should be eating three times the amount she normally eats. Ensure that fresh, clean water is always available for her near the whelping box.

How do I know whether my dog is producing adequate milk, and if she isn't, how and what should I feed the hungry puppies?

Some female dogs are not able to produce an adequate quantity of milk, and the puppies remain hungry. Feed them milk formula (meant for babies) in a special puppy feeding bottle, every two hours. Feeding them with a dropper or spoon is difficult and should be avoided. However, it is very important that they first get their mother's milk (colostrum), which contains antibodies to protect them from infections until their own immune system becomes functional. Several commercial dog food manufacturers now make milk formulas for puppies, and special feeds for pregnant and lactating female dogs. These are quite good and can be safely given to the puppies and their mother.

How should one look after orphan puppies if their mother dies?

Orphan puppies require special attention, as they have to be fed with milk-formula diets, initially every two hours. Their ano-genital region needs to be cleaned several times a day with cotton wool moistened with water, to stimulate them to urinate and defecate. To keep them warm, wrap a hot-water bottle in a towel and place it in the whelping box. An infra-red lamp may also be required during the severe winter months. After feeding them, wipe the milk from their mouths and bodies. Handle them frequently, cleaning their eyes, ears and mouth at least twice a day with cotton wool moistened with warm water.

Sometimes some weak puppies cannot suckle, and the mother also does not allow them to do so. What should one do in such a situation?

Pick up the puppy carefully, and while talking to the mother (telling her to be a good dog) squeeze her nipple gently, drawing some milk. Open the puppy's mouth, help him catch hold of the nipple and suckle. Keep talking to the dog, as she will feel ticklish when the puppy suckles for the first time. This may be due to the excessive engorgement of the mammary glands with milk, which causes discomfort. She will feel better after you squeeze out some milk manually.

What common problems do female dogs face after whelping?

Infection of the uterus (metritis) due to a retained placenta, or a dead puppy, is the most common problem faced by female dogs after whelping. It is a serious condition, with fever, loss of appetite and sometimes vomiting, and needs to be treated immediately by a vet. Inflammation of the mammary glands (mastitis) is another problem, this caused by bacterial infection. The symptoms are pain and swelling, and the mother does not allow her puppies to suckle. In such a situation, the puppies will require hand-feeding, and the mother will have to be treated by a vet. Sometimes, due to calcium deficiency after whelping, a female dog may develop milk fever (eclampsia), which is accompanied by disorientation, convulsions and collapse. This is common in small dogs that have a large litter. Such cases respond to intravenous calcium therapy, which can only be administered by a vet.

At what age should puppies be given solid food?

Puppies get their milk teeth by the time they are six weeks old. They can then eat solid food and are ready to be weaned.

Why does a female dog snap at her puppies while suckling them when they are around five to six weeks old?

She does not produce adequate milk for her puppies after they are five weeks old. Moreover, while suckling, the puppies hurt her mammary glands with their sharp milk teeth. She gets irritated and starts snapping at them.

Should puppies be dewormed by the breeder? If so at what age?

Almost all puppies contract worm infestation from their mother, either during the pre-natal stage, or through the mother's milk after birth. Deworm them at four weeks, and then at weekly intervals under veterinary supervision.

Should the puppies be given a bath if they get dirty?

Puppies should not be bathed till they are three months old. Regularly brush their coats, and clean their eyes, ears and mouth with wet cotton wool.

Do puppies need to get their nails clipped?

Puppies scratch their mother's breasts, causing painful swelling. Clip the sharp tips of their nails with a pair of scissors when they are three to four weeks old.

Should puppies be fed together or individually?

Always feed puppies together so that they learn to share and are not possessive about their food as adults.

How does one monitor the growth and weight gain of the puppies?

Carefully monitor the weight gain of each puppy every day. The weak puppies, or those not gaining the desired weight, may have to be physically helped to suck milk from the more productive teats, which are at the rear end of the udder.

At what age should one start grooming the puppies?

Start grooming them when they are four weeks old. Puppies of long-haired breeds can be groomed when they are three weeks old. Early grooming teaches a puppy to be obedient and disciplined.

Birth Control, Spaying and Neutering

Female dogs undergo ovario-hysterectomy (spaying) as a birth-control measure. This is a major surgery carried out under general anaesthesia, and both the ovaries and the uterus are removed. Although they can be spayed at any age, for best results it should be done before they attain puberty, when they are five or six months old. Spaying is common in foreign countries to check the birth of unwanted puppies.

In the case of male dogs, castration is carried out as a birth-control measure, and both the testicles are surgically removed. This is called neutering. Neutering can be done at any age but is recommended when the dog is about six to seven months old, before it attains puberty. This surgery is also done under general anaesthesia, but it is not a major operation.

What are the main advantages of getting a female dog spayed?

A spayed female dog will never have her season, or a false pregnancy, and will not breed. Besides, she is unlikely to get mammary tumours and an infection of the uterus known as metritis or pyometra in old age. Many un-spayed female dogs suffer from these problems (which can be life-threatening if they are not treated in time) after they are seven or eight years old. Spaying makes a female dog gentler, especially if she has a tendency to be aggressive and dominating.

Does spaying have any side-effects?

A spayed female dog puts on weight if she is not exercised regularly. Her calorie intake should be reduced by ten percent after the operation.

Is it possible to prevent a female dog from having her season without getting her spayed?

It is possible to postpone her season by giving her oral hormone pills. However, these have undesirable side-effects, and hence are not recommended.

What should one do if a female dog mis-mates during her season?

Immediately take her to the vet, who will administer a hormonal injection and also douche the uterus. This will prolong the season. However, if another mating takes place subsequently, she will conceive. Be very careful and ensure that she does not mis-mate again. This procedure is not a hundred per cent effective. The best way of avoiding accidental mis-mating is to get a female dog spayed.

What are the advantages of having a male dog neutered?

Neutering curbs undesirable behaviour in a male dog, such as mounting people's legs, hyper-excitability and over-aggressiveness. A neutered male dog does not keep running away from home after a female dog in season, and is generally more disciplined. Also he does not also get the urge to urine-mark his territory.

What are the side-effects of neutering in a male dog?

A neutered dog becomes quieter and tends to put on weight if he is inadequately exercised and his calorie intake is not reduced by ten per cent.

Are neutered dogs able to mate?

Till such time as the male hormone (testosterone) level does not come down, neutered dogs may have the urge to mate.

How can I prevent mis-mating and unwanted pregnancies in my female dog without spaying her?

When she is in season, do not take her out of the house without a leash. She should be strictly supervised at all times during this period. Do not let her come in contact with male dogs. If you are not interested in breeding her, get her spayed. There are long-acting hormonal injections available which prevent the onset of oestrous up to a year. These, however, should be used judiciously because of possible side-effects.

Can a male dog be vasectomized?

A male dog can be vasectomized. This will not change his character in any way, or cause him to gain weight.

Correcting Bad Habits and Behaviour

There are certain habits, such as the pack instinct, which dogs have inherited from their ancestors, the wolves. Other habits acquired by them—some good, and some bad—are often the result of unpleasant experiences. Dogs rescued from bad homes invariably suffer from behavioural problems. These manifest themselves in many ways, such as the desire to eat excreta, biting, attacking people, excessive barking, chewing things, begging, jumping on people or chasing them, and scavenging in garbage pails. Owning a badly-behaved dog with unpleasant habits is a big liability and one should make an effort to understand one's dog in

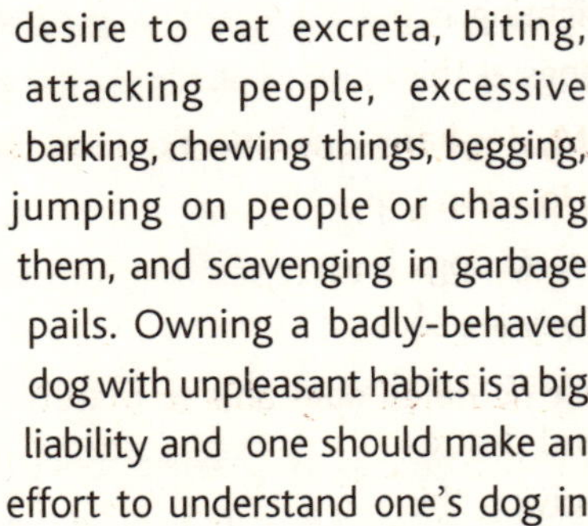

order to identify his problems and take corrective action. A dog can also inherit some behavioural problems from his pedigree or breed. Most of these problems, however, are the result of mishandling, bad training and carelessness on the part of owners. Some, such as urinating in the house, may be linked to an underlying medical cause. Behavioural problems in dogs can be corrected by the judicious use of verbal reprimands, frightening them with unexpected sounds, and if required, by physical isolation for a few minutes. Never be lax about discipline, and if you face these problems, discuss them with your vet.

When dogs fight, do they bite or injure each other?

In most cases there is little likelihood of serious injury. The dominant dog may snap at his rival, but fights are generally brief, and the loser beats a hasty retreat.

How do I know in advance if my dog is going to pick a fight with another dog?

Dogs send a series of coded signals to each other based on body language. This is to make the weaker dog back out from the fight. As they intend to intimidate, they make themselves look as large as possible. They growl menacingly, and as the situation intensifies and fighting is imminent, they bare their teeth. You must separate the dogs at this juncture in order to prevent a fight.

My dog barks continuously when I go out. This annoys my neighbours. How can I stop this?

Many dogs bark continuously in protest when they are left alone. They are sociable animals, and when left alone in the house, become agitated and frustrated. Apart from barking, they may also chew, bite and destroy things, and defecate and urinate in the house as well. Solving this problem requires patience and understanding. You will

have to train your dog to remain quiet when he is left alone. From a young age, give the command, 'QUIET', and pretend you are going out. Stay close to the house, and see if the dog barks. If he does, go back immediately and scold him, again giving the command 'QUIET' or 'NO'. Otherwise, before going out, put the dog in a portable kennel or crate. He will regard it as his own room and will not defecate or urinate inside it. You can keep one of your used clothes inside it. The scent of your body will comfort your dog when he is alone. Practise leaving him alone in the crate or kennel for short periods (for about ten to fifteen minutes), and praise him if he remains quiet. To keep him occupied, give him some chewable toys to play with. Leaving a TV or radio on in the house is comforting and reduces separation anxiety in dogs. Electronic bark collars are used in western countries to prevent excessive barking.

Why do dogs chew things?

Puppies love to chew things when they are teething. Many older dogs also do this for fun, due to boredom, and sometimes because of excessive energy. Dogs chew objects when left alone, or when nobody is watching them. If you catch your dog doing this, or gnawing at furniture, it is time for you to get him chewable toys such as a rubber bone, a ball, etc. When he plays with his toys, praise him; but scold him, immediately by saying 'NO', if he reverts to chewing or gnawing. Adequate exercise and regular obedience training will help in controlling most bad habits such as chewing. Also discuss this problem with your vet.

Why do some pet dogs bite people?

Some dogs have the bad habit of biting people, which is a cause for embarrassment to the dog's owner. Guarding his territory against all

intruders is a dog's natural instinct. Ferocious breeds may attack or bite if not properly trained. Most often, a dog bites because he is being teased or annoyed. Children should be told never to tease or bother the dog, especially when he is sleeping or eating. On the other hand, saying 'NO' or 'VERY BAD' in a firm tone should immediately check any aggressive behaviour on the part of the dog.

Why do some dogs beg when people are eating?

This bad habit is the result of table scraps being fed to the dog by his owner. Initially this is done merely to pamper him, but when there are guests eating, and the dog starts demanding food, this is very embarrassing for the owner. However, it is the owner's fault in the first place! Never ever offer titbits to your dog. In fact, feed him before the family sits down to eat. When he begs, scold him and put him in his box or kennel. Eventually he will learn that begging does not pay.

How can dogs be prevented from jumping on visitors?

This is an embarrassing and annoying habit, especially for visitors who do not like dogs. They may feel frightened, and the dog may even dirty or tear their clothes. In order to stop this, never pat your dog or give him a treat when he jumps on you. Put him on a leash, and whenever he jumps on you, firmly say 'NO', and give his leash a sideways jerk. Order him to sit down, and when he does, praise him effusively. Another way to avoid this nuisance is to shut the dog in an indoor kennel or in another room till the visitors leave.

Some dogs chase cars and cycles. How can this bad habit be corrected?

This is a dangerous habit and can cause serious accidents. Corrective action should be taken the moment you find your dog tempted to chase a moving car, cycle or human being. Never take him out without a leash. The moment he makes an attempt to chase anything or anyone, sharply jerk his leash and say 'NO' firmly. After this is done several times he will know that what he is trying to do is wrong.

It is very embarrassing when my dog mounts my leg in front of guests. How do I correct this bad habit?

To correct this habit, the moment your dog or puppy mounts your leg, catch hold of his collar firmly, and at the same time say 'NO' firmly. Then push him aside. This should be repeated every time he does it.

My puppy sometimes eats his own faeces. How can I stop him from doing this?

Many puppies eat their faeces soon after defecating. This can be due to various causes, such as the puppy being very hungry; a deficiency of digestive enzymes, trace elements and minerals; or because of worm infestation. Discuss this problem with your vet, who will examine all the aspects of the problem and advise you regarding remedial measures. Deworm the puppy monthly with broad-spectrum anthelmintics, and give him yeast with osto calcium syrup, as a preventive measure. Reprimand the puppy with a firm 'NO' or 'VERY BAD', immediately, if he is caught in the act of eating faeces, and catch him by his collar and give him a shake. Put kerosene oil on the faeces it will effectively prevent him from eating it.

Checklist for Correcting Bad Habits and Behaviour

- Boredom and loneliness encourage a dog to develop destructive habits.
- Daily exercise depletes excess energy and prevents the dog from picking up bad habits.

- Check your dog at once with a firm 'NO' if you catch him doing something wrong.
- Do not give titbits or table scraps to your dog.
- Do not allow him to climb on sofas or beds.
- Never ever hit your dog to correct bad habits.
- Regularly deworm your dog and feed him a balanced diet with trace elements and minerals.
- Reward him generously when he responds positively to a reprimand.
- Do not breed your dog with one that has incurable and genetically-linked bad habits, or one that bites.
- Do not leave your dog alone for a long time.
- Always be gentle and loving with him.

Tick and Flea Control

Ticks and fleas are a cause of great discomfort to a dog. They suck their host's blood and are responsible for transmitting several serious diseases. They are skin parasites and can be seen with the naked eye. Ticks are very common ectoparasites in tropical countries. They are voracious bloodsuckers and are the most difficult of all skin parasites to get rid of. Warm and moist climatic conditions favour their multiplication. Apart from the dog's body, they also live in grass, bushes, and in cracks and crevices in the house, hibernating during the winter months.

Fleas are very small, dark brown bloodsucking parasites, almost the size of

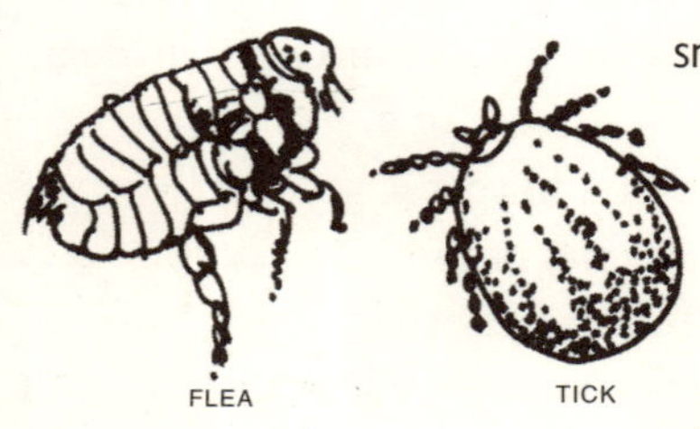

small ants. They live on the bodies of dogs and cats. They cause severe irritation and itching, leading to dermatitis. They also transmit several viral diseases, and act as intermediary hosts for dog tapeworms.

What is the life cycle of ticks?

After mating on the body of the dog, the female tick drops off and hides in cracks and crevices in the house to lay eggs. After a couple of weeks, a large number of baby ticks appear and attach themselves to the dog to suck blood. Ticks are prolific breeders and can survive for months hiding in cracks and crevices.

What are the common symptoms of a tick infestation?

Dogs infested with ticks scratch themselves constantly, and suffer from hair loss and skin eruptions. On examining the area, you will find that it is infested with ticks. Generally, ticks choose places which are inaccessible to the dog, such as inside the ears, between the paws, under the neck and belly, and around the anus.

How do ticks harm dogs?

Ticks suck blood, and in a heavy infestation, can cause anemia. They cause intense irritation, constant itching and are a source of intense discomfort to the dog. They also transmit deadly diseases, such as Piroplasmosis (tick fever) and Ehrlichiosis, in dogs.

How can one prevent tick infestation?

During the daily grooming schedule, carefully check for the presence of ticks. Remove them with tweezers, put them in a small container of kerosene oil, and then burn them. Daily de-ticking is the most

effective method of controlling tick infestation. During the summer months and the rainy season, when ticks multiply very fast, use tick repellents such as anti-tick powder, and bathe your dog with an anti-tick shampoo. For severe infections, after bathing your dog, apply a strong anti-tick medicated lotion, such as Butox and Ridd, under the guidance of your vet. Apart from destroying the ticks on the dog's body, one should also pay attention to those hidden in the house.

Are ticks a threat to human beings?

Apart from biting human beings, ticks can transmit certain diseases such as Lyme's disease (which has been reported in the USA), which causes arthritis and neurological complications.

How does one detect a flea infestation in a dog?

A dog infected with fleas keeps biting his skin, particularly on the tail. Fleas cause severe irritation and itching, leading to dermatitis, and red spots appear on the body. On close examination, one can see tiny dark specks in the dog's fur. This is flea-faeces, which is digested blood. You can even see adult fleas, very small dark brown creatures, moving very fast in the fur.

What is the life cycle of a flea?

There are four stages in the life cycle of a dog flea: egg, larva, pupa and the adult flea. The time taken to complete a life cycle varies from a

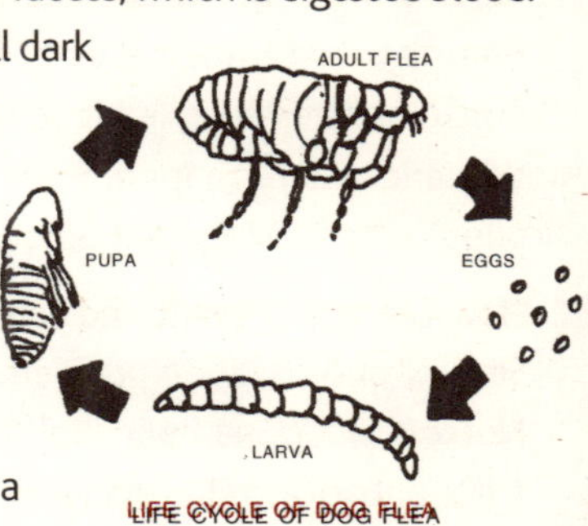

LIFE CYCLE OF DOG FLEA

month to a year, depending on the temperature, moisture and availability of food. The life span of a flea varies from six to twelve months, and during its lifetime it lays several hundred eggs. These eggs fall off the dog's fur and complete their life cycle away from him.

How do fleas infect dogs?

Fleas can jump from one dog to another. Apart from that, new adult fleas (from eggs which have fallen off their fur) infect them. Even if the owner and his dog are away from the house for a while, fleas-eggs, which have fallen on carpets, furniture and the dog's bedding, survive and grow into adult fleas when the dog returns, as they need blood to survive and multiply.

Do fleas attach themselves to human beings?

Dog fleas also bite human beings and suck their blood.

How do fleas harm dogs?

They cause intense itching and allergic dermatitis, accompanied by red patches on the skin and loss of hair, especially on the tail. The dog becomes restless, unhealthy and constantly bites and scratches his body. Fleas also act as intermediary hosts for a species of dog tapeworms. Their saliva contains an antigen and an allergen, which is then injected into the body of the dog, causing intense itching. Constant scratching leads to a secondary bacterial infection of the skin and pus formation. Fleas can cause severe anaemia in young puppies by sucking their blood.

How can one prevent and control tick and flea infestation in dogs?

Several anti-tick/flea powders, sprays and shampoos are available: Notix Powder/Shampoo, Bolfo Spray/Shampoo, Asuntol Powder and Kiltix anti-tick collar made by Bayer; Butox made by Hoechst; Ridd

made by Petcare, and Cisaflux Shampoo made by Ranbaxy. All these should be used under veterinary guidance. Utilize pest control services to destroy the pupa and the young fleas on the carpets and furniture in the house. Get the dog's bedding and the floor of the house vacuumed periodically. The bedding should also be washed sometimes as an additional precaution. Use a flea comb when grooming your dog, and deworm him against tapeworms regularly if he is infested with fleas.

What is the role of fleas in the spread of dog tapeworms?

A dog sheds the eggs of tapeworms that are within his body in his faeces, which sometimes stick to his fur. A flea ingests these eggs, which further develop in its body. When the dog scratches himself because of intense irritation caused by the fleas, he accidentally swallows the flea containing the developing stages of the tapeworm, and thus gets re-infected with this infection.

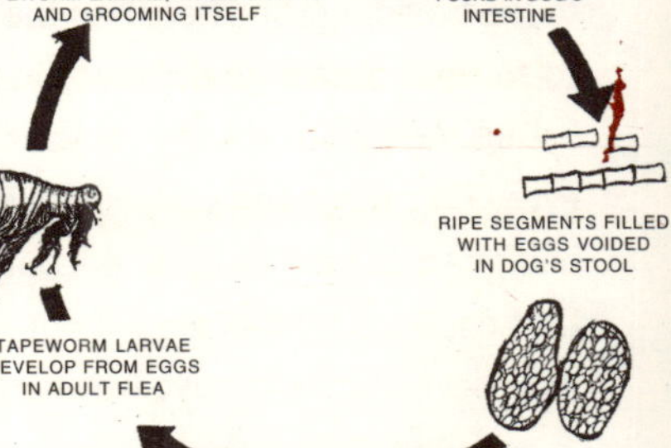

LIFE CYCLE OF DOG TAPEWORM

Checklist for Flea and Tick Control

- Groom your dog every day and manually remove the ticks with tweezers.
- Use anti-tick/flea powders after grooming, especially inside the paws, during summer and the rainy season.

- Bathe your dog every month in summer with an anti-tick/flea shampoo.
- Have the house treated for pest control if there is a heavy infestation of ticks/fleas.
- Keep your dog's bedding clean.
- Consult your vet and seek his advice about how you should deal with a heavy tick or flea infestation.
- Deworm your dog periodically, as advised by your vet.

Exercise and Training

In order to keep one's dog healthy and happy, it is essential to exercise him regularly. The actual amount of exercise needed varies according to the breed, age and health of the dog. Inadequate or no exercise leads to several diseases which can be prevented, as in the case of human beings. Adequate exercise means a thirty to forty-minute brisk walk every day. Dogs enjoy playing with each other and also with human beings so they should be encouraged, as playing is also an exercise that depletes their energy. If your dog is not adequately exercised, he may develop destructive habits to use up his excess energy.

Training dogs is an ongoing process, and refresher training is essential for all adult dogs. However, if your dog was not trained at the age of five to six months he will take much longer to learn obedience-training commands. It requires great patience to train adult dogs that have not been exposed to basic obedience training, as they form certain behavioural patterns which have to be broken. During and after their daily exercise, dogs should be put through a fixed training routine, so that they do not forget what they have learnt. To correct bad habits, the services of a professional trainer are required.

How many times during the day should one take one's dog out?

Walk your dog for thirty to forty minutes or alternatively take him out twice or thrice a day for short walks. This will enhance his quality of life, and will also satisfy curiosity about his surroundings.

What is the best way of taking one's dog out for a walk?

Always take your dog out on a leash with a collar. However, a harness can also be used instead of a leash. Small dogs should be fitted with a harness, as it is less stressful for them.

How does one control a dog that is aggressive towards other dogs during exercise?

Muzzle an aggressive dog during exercise. An over-aggressive dog should be neutered. This will diminish his aggressiveness.

What precautions should one take while exercising one's dog during the summer, winter and rainy season?

Excessive exercise in hot weather can cause heatstroke or heat exhaustion. Dogs have a few sweat glands between their toes and their only other way of losing heat is by the evaporation of fluids from their nasal mucosa. Therefore, they are more prone to heat stress than humans. Never exercise your dog excessively during hot weather. In cold and wet weather, a warm or waterproof coat is recommended to ensure that he does not get wet.

Should I allow my dog to run free, in addition to his regular exercise?

Dogs enjoy a free run. However, make sure that your dog is at liberty in a confined and fenced area, so that he does not run off. An extendable leash will enable him to enjoy partial freedom.

Is swimming a good exercise for dogs?

Dogs, especially Retrievers, love swimming. However, they cannot swim against a strong current, so do not allow your dog to swim in a rough sea, a stream, or canal with fast currents.

Should one give toys to dogs?

Dogs love playing with toys and should be encouraged to do so. You must, however, train your dog to always drop any toy on command.

Should I allow my dog to play with other pet dogs?

Dogs enjoy playing with each other. Let your dog play with other immunized and dewormed pet dogs.

Is it safe to throw sticks for dogs to retrieve?

No, it is not; it could injure their eyes or mouths. Always throw plastic or rubber toys for your dog to retrieve. This is an excellent way of exercising him with the least effort expended.

What should I do if my dog disappears during exercise?

Call out his name loudly, asking him to come to you. In most cases, he will find his way to the house if he is familiar with the walking route. If a female dog in season attracts your dog, he may not heed your command, and could disappear for a couple of days. During this time, he will probably fight with stray dogs, and may return badly wounded, perhaps even infected with rabies. If you have a male dog, handle him very carefully when there are female dogs in season around.

What should I do if my dog is lost?

Report the loss to the local police and search the neighbouring area thoroughly, calling him by his name. Inform the vets in your neighbourhood, giving full details of his appearance, breed, age, sex and colour.

How should one go about giving refresher training to an adult dog that has been given basic obedience training as a puppy?

Adult dogs need to undergo regular refresher obedience training otherwise they tend to forget what they have learnt during their

basic training. Dogs learn by repetition so spend ten to fifteen minutes every day imparting refresher training to your dog after his morning walk, before grooming him. Do this before feeding him, so that he is more responsive to the training and looks forward to his reward. Repeat the basic commands, 'SIT', 'DOWN', 'LIE DOWN', 'STAY', 'COME', 'HEEL' and 'SPEAK' every day. Always encourage your dog with verbal praise, or by giving him a treat when he obeys the commands.

What is the modern concept regarding canine obedience training?

Kindness, patience and understanding get better results than punishment when training a dog.

Is verbal and physical praise as effective as a treat?

Praise, whether verbal (appreciative words) or physical (petting), is very important. It encourages the dog during training and reassures him when his response is positive. It is as good as a treat.

Can any member of the family train the dog?

Yes, the dog's response will be the same if he is equally attached to all the members of the family. However, most dogs respect and love one person more than others, and this is invariably the head of the family.

What are the common problems encountered during training?

If a dog is not properly conditioned for training, he may be uninterested and ignore commands. If this is so, be firm with him. Do not allow him to get away without being disciplined during the training. Firmness, with kindness and patience, is the key to success in dog training. However, some dogs that have not been trained as puppies may need the help of a professional dog trainer to discipline them. Take the help of your vet in finding a suitable dog trainer.

Travelling With Your Dog

Travelling with your dog requires careful planning, whether it is by road, rail, sea or air. The preparations required for each mode of travel are different. Invariably long-distance travel by any mode of transport is a stressful experience for animals. However, most dogs love an outing in a car. Travelling with your dog, if he is properly trained, and if the journey is well planned, can be an enjoyable experience.

What precautions should be taken when travelling with a dog by car?

Some dogs get car-sick and vomit when travelling in a car. If your dog has this problem, feed him at least two hours before starting on the journey and do not give him water for at least an hour before. Administer anti- vomiting oral medication at least thirty minutes before starting off. Stop every few hours, take the dog out to answer the call of nature, and offer him some water while he is outside the car. Never leave your dog in the car with doors and windows shut. Dogs can suffer from heatstroke (which can be fatal) if they are locked inside a car in hot weather.

What precautions should be taken while transporting a dog by rail?

The railway authorities in India allow dogs to travel in a kennel in the guard's compartment. A small dog may be allowed to travel with his owner (if he is travelling by First Class AC/First Class), provided other passengers do not object. The dog has to be properly immunized and dewormed before the journey. The kennel in the guard's compartment should be cleaned and disinfected if your dog is going to travel in it. Take him out to urinate and defecate, and for short walks at stations where the train stops for a long time. Provide clean water for the dog (preferably in his own bowl), and give him light food during the journey. During cold weather, make sure that he has proper bedding and a coat. Visit the dog often in order to reassure him. If your dog has an aggressive temperament, he may need a sedative and a muzzle while travelling.

What precautions should one take when transporting a dog by sea?

Like humans, some dogs tend to be seasick, and they may require treatment with anti-nausea drugs. Many dogs also have a problem in getting used to defecating on board, and become constipated. A mild laxative and regular walking are recommended for them.

What precautions should one take when transporting a dog by air?

Transporting a dog by air has to be planned after consulting the airline one is travelling with. Remember that a veterinary health certificate is required for international travel. Dogs have to be properly immunized in advance, and are kept in portable kennels during air shipment. The size and type of kennel required is intimated by the airline. It should have adequate space for the dog to move about in and turn. Some dogs may require a sedative, which also acts as an anti-nausea medicine, before starting on the journey. If your dog is travelling by air, give him food and water at least two hours before the flight. Ensure that fresh, clean water is provided for him in his kennel. The airline staff will check up on him during stopovers.

Preparing for a Dog Show

Various Kennel Clubs and societies in India arrange dog shows. Most of these shows are open to specific breeds of pedigreed dogs that are registered with their respective Kennel Clubs. Only registered dogs are allowed to participate in obedience competitions. Pure-bred dogs are compared with laid-down breed standards to find the perfect specimen amongst the competing dogs. A dog is judged for his body shape, general appearance, coat colour, temperament, and the way he deports himself in the show ring. He loses points for any deviation from the breed standard.

There are several criteria for entering a dog in a dog show. The dog must be in good health (and vaccinated), as he may contract contagious/infectious diseases at the show, or pass on his ailments to other dogs. His appearance must be immaculate as a result of good grooming, and he should be well trained and well behaved so that he does not disturb fellow competitors.

It is advisable for a prospective show-dog owner to attend as many dog shows as possible to watch dog handlers. He should observe keenly how various breeds are shown and then emulate the dog handlers during practice sessions.

How should one prepare one's dog for the show?

It takes a few months to prepare a dog for a dog show. Groom your dog everyday and bathe him the day before the show; for long-haired breeds, take the help of an experienced dog trainer or a professional who grooms long-haired dogs for shows. Daily exercise and good nutrition is imperative to get your dog into shape for the competition. Register him in the specific class or breed category he is eligible for. This can be verified from the show brochure. Discuss the important points with your vet, especially those pertaining to health and vaccinations.

What points should I bear in mind before taking my dog into the ring?

Encourage him to urinate or defecate before entering the ring. Make sure that your show entry number is clearly visible, and that your clothes complement your dog's appearance. Finally, check him to ensure that he is fit in every way.

How does one train an excitable and temperamental dog for a show?

Good behaviour is a criterion for a prospective champion or winner. If your dog is excitable and highly strung, he will disturb other dogs by barking at them, and will not allow the judge to examine him properly. This problem can be overcome by training him, and letting him socialize with other pet dogs as often as possible. You can also take the help of a professional dog trainer.

What kind of training is required for a dog to participate in a dog show?

You must train the dog to respond to basic commands, especially to walk at heel without pulling ahead or dragging behind. He should also be so well trained that he ignores his fellow competitors and is not distracted by them.

How can one increase the chances of one's dog winning at a show?

Ensure that your dog is well-trained, groomed, presented correctly, and that he is a good, healthy specimen of his breed. Enrol him in preparatory classes so that he learns how to behave with other competitors, is totally relaxed, and develops a proper show temperament.

Can one predict whether a puppy will be a future champion?

A well-bred and pedigreed puppy, born of champion parents conforming to breed standards, who has been properly trained and looked after, has the potential of becoming a champion. Take expert advice regarding the future prospects of a puppy you wish to buy.

What is meant by the term 'champion' on the pedigree sheet?

The term 'champion' is used for a dog that has won three challenge certificates under three different judges of a particular Kennel Club. After having achieved this unique feat, the CH is added to his name in the pedigree sheet.

How does a judge select the winner?

Each competitor is assessed for his trueness to laid-down breed standards. The judge minutely examines him and his general conduct, turnout and movements are all important points that are taken into consideration.

3

elderly dogs

As animals age their needs change. Older dogs sleep more, prefer shorter walks, and are less active. The average life span of a dog is approximately twelve years. Smaller breeds such as Chihuahuas, miniature Dachshunds and toy Poodles have a longer life span and may live up to fifteen or seventeen years. Larger breeds such as Great Danes, St. Bernards and Afghan Hounds have a comparatively shorter life span, ranging from ten to fourteen years. The life expectancy of dogs has increased in recent years, with better health and veterinary care.

CARE, MANAGEMENT AND PROBLEMS OF ELDERLY DOGS

The external signs of ageing are graying hair on and around the muzzle, deterioration of hearing and eyesight, muscle shrinkage, weakening of the body, and thinning and trying of the coat. The ageing process varies with every dog, and depends to a large extent on nutrition, exercise and the environment. As with humans, you may not notice the ageing process in some dogs as much as in others. An old dog gradually becomes lethargic and slow. With regular check-ups, a special diet, regular light exercise and gentle grooming you can make his life comfortable.

How does one take care of an old dog?

An old dog needs extra care as far as diet, grooming, massaging of stiff joints and dental care are concerned. The eyes and ears also need special care.

What should the diet of an elderly dog consist of?

The ability of the digestive tract to digest and absorb nutrients slows down with age. Therefore, the quantity and quality of an elderly dog's diet needs to be adjusted accordingly. He should consume about twenty per cent less calories to maintain his weight, and as he is normally unable to chew his food properly due to age-related dental problems, his food should be soft and easily digestible. Special dog foods for elderly dogs are commercially manufactured; they are specially prepared keeping their requirements in mind. Elderly dogs have a tendency to get constipated, so more fibre should be included in their diet.

How should I look after my dog's failing eyesight?

An elderly dog's eyes should be cleaned with a piece of damp cotton wool every day because they get coated with excess mucous. Also clean the skin around the eyes. Most old dogs develop cataracts. Dogs with advanced cataract become blind, but they are still able to manage quite well with their well-developed sense of smell and memory of the layout of the house. Never let a blind dog roam freely outside the house. Make sure he is always taken out on a leash, and do not change the layout of the furniture and fixtures as this will help him find his way around the house. Ensure that his water and food bowls are always there in the place they are normally kept. Including Vitamins A and D in your dog's diet will help in delaying cataract formation.

Should any special care be taken to look after the ears of an elderly dog?

An elderly dog's ears need periodic cleaning by a vet to remove the wax and check for ear infection, which is an old-age problem. A

dog's hearing is often impaired as he grows older, and some dogs become totally deaf after reaching the age of twelve or thirteen. If your dog does not come to greet you at the door when you return home it is a sign that his hearing is impaired. In such a case, consult your vet immediately. Never let a deaf dog loose outside the house, as he will not be able to respond to your commands. However, as he can feel ground vibrations, you can tap the ground to draw his attention.

How should one care for an elderly dog's teeth and gums?

Like humans, elderly dogs also have dental problems, and if there are no regular check-ups and scaling of teeth by a vet, they are likely to suffer from severe inflammation of the gums due to accumulation of tartar, which, in turn, leads to bacterial infection. This causes bad breath and constant salivation, they are unable to eat properly, and lose condition. They emit a foul odour from their mouths, which gradually becomes unbearable. Take your elderly dog to a vet for regular dental treatment to prevent this from happening.

Can an old dog be fitted with dentures?

It is not possible to train a dog to wear and use dentures like humans. Preventive dental care is therefore the best option for them.

What should be kept in mind when grooming an elderly dog?

As a dog ages, his skin and hair coat becomes thinner and more sensitive, therefore he needs a softer brush and gentle grooming. His anal glands should be checked regularly to prevent the development of peri-anal fistulas.

How does one massage the stiff joints of an elderly dog?

Most elderly dogs develop arthritic changes in the joints. Arthritis is a slow and progressive disease, which causes stiffness and discomfort in dogs and hampers their movement. Arthritic changes show up sooner if the dog has not been regularly exercised over the years. Elderly dogs' stiff joints should be massaged, especially after rest, sleep, and during the winter months, when the problem is aggravated. Lightly massage the muscles and joints when the dog is relaxing. Exercise the limb joints gently through flexion and extension. In painful joint conditions, oral medication with Aspirin and non-steroidal anti-inflammatory drugs helps. Consult your vet regarding an advanced and very painful case of arthritis.

Do old dogs also suffer from diabetes and heart problems? How can one prevent these disorders?

As with humans, many dogs develop diabetes, which can cause premature cataract. They also suffer from heart diseases, with symptoms such as constant coughing, breathing difficulties, and tiring easily. Smaller dogs are predisposed to myocardial infarction (deadening of the heart muscle caused by hardening of the arteries), and larger dogs to atrial fibrillation (persistent interruption of the normal heart rhythm, often fatal). Such dogs need special dietary and veterinary care, and diagnostic tests, including X-rays.

Most elderly dogs become obese. How can one prevent this?

Overfeeding and lack of exercise cause obesity. It is common in elderly female dogs. Obese dogs face the same health risks as humans. They have a shorter life span and often suffer from diabetes, arthritis, and liver, kidney, lung and heart problems. They get tired quickly and are short of breath. Such dogs are poor anaesthetic risks and have a low resistance to infections. Regular, gentle exercise with dietary control

will help in improving fitness levels and reduce weight. A low-fat, high-fibre diet with fewer calories is best for obese dogs, however special dog food for obese dogs is not available commercially. If your dog is obese, exercise him two or three times a day by taking him for short walks without tiring him. Do not give him any table scraps, remove leftover food immediately after his meal, and exercise him more. Consult your vet about tackling the problem.

OBESE

What are the signs of obesity in a dog?

A grossly obese dog is easily noticeable. To detect obesity, run your hands over the rib cage of the dog, on both sides (standing behind him), and also feel the bones at the base of his tail. If the outline of the ribs and bones cannot be felt, the dog is obese, and you should take steps to reduce his weight.

OVERWEIGHT

What is the difference between an overweight and an obese dog?

IDEAL WEIGHT

You will be able to feel the ribs of an overweight dog by pressing his rib cage, and palpate the bones at the base of his tail, under a moderate layer of fat. His abdomen will be almost straight, but not tucked in. On the other hand, the abdomen of an obese dog will be flabby and will hang down, and you will find it difficult to feel the ribs and palpate the bones at the base of the tail, because of the accumulation of excess fat on them.

Are some breeds more prone to obesity?

Labradors, Beagles and Dachshunds are most prone to obesity.

Do neutering and spaying make dogs obese?

Yes, to an extent. Care should be taken not to overfeed neutered males and spayed female dogs. They should also be adequately and regularly exercised.

Are elderly dogs more prone to tumours/cancers?

Elderly dogs have a higher incidence of tumours/cancers. Mammary tumours in elderly females and testicular tumours in elderly male dogs are common. As a precaution, even a small growth on a dog's body should be taken seriously and surgically removed before it increases in size and spreads. Early neutering and spaying prevents mammary and testicular tumours.

Some elderly dogs lose control over their bowel and bladder movements. What should one do if this happens?

They should be taken out of the house more frequently, and preferably be confined in a specific area, which can be easily cleaned. Veterinary help and dietary change may help in minimizing the problem.

Is it true that one dog year equals seven human years, and that according to this equation a ten-year-old dog is the same age as a seventy-year-old human being?

Although dogs age much faster than humans, the simple equation of one canine year being equivalent to seven human years is not always true. According to the latest research, the equation/interpretation of

a dog's year vis-à-vis that of a human being depends on the size and weight of the dog. For example, a six-year-old dog weighing up to ten kilograms is the same age as a forty-year-old man; if he weighs between eleven and twenty-five kilograms, he is as old as a forty-two-year-old human. If his weight is between twenty-six and forty kilograms, he is equal in age to a forty-five-year-old person. The corresponding age of dogs with that of human beings is given on page 120.

What is the longest life span recorded for a dog?

The longest recorded age of a dog is twenty-nine years.

What age-related behavioural problems do elderly dogs suffer from?

Older dogs are less tolerant of being teased by children. They also suffer from separation anxiety, inappropriate elimination, and aggression towards people, increased vocalization and sensitivity to noise. Reduced blood and oxygen supply to the brain can cause a serious problem known as cognitive disorder. This is characterized by a decreased reaction to stimuli, and causes dogs to not recognize members of the family or old friends. It can also cause disorientation in their movements, increased irritability, and inability to sleep at night, decreased attentiveness or staring into space. This disorder responds to medication, which has to be administered through the dog's life.

Signs of ageing in dogs

- Graying muzzle
- Clouding of the eyes
- A slightly stiff gait
- Weight gain
- Impaired vision and hearing

- Greater susceptibility to illness
- Increased irritability

Geriatric Help line

- Daily walking
- Regular veterinary check-ups and blood tests
- Regular vaccinations
- Regular parasitic check-ups for fleas/ticks/internal parasites/worms
- Controlled feeding to maintain optimum weight
- Gentle grooming

***

Age Equation of Adult Dogs in Human Years

Age of Dog	Body weight of dog			
	Up to 10 kg	11 - 25 kg	26 - 40 kg	Over 40 kg
	Corresponding Age of Human Beings			
6 years	40 years	42 years	45 years	49 years
7 years	44 years	47 years	50 years	56 years
8 years	48 years	51 years	54 years	63 years
9 years	52 years	56 years	61 years	71 years
10 years	56 years	60 years	66 years	78 years
11 years	60 years	65 years	72 years	86 years
12 years	64 years	69 years	77 years	93 years
13 years	68 years	74 years	82 years	101 years
14 years	72 years	78 years	88 years	108 years
15 years	76 years	83 years	93 years	115 years
16 years	80 years	87 years	99 years	123 years

preventive health care, first aid, diseases and home remedies

Due to advances in veterinary science, pet dogs now have a longer life span. Most serious and fatal contagious/infectious diseases have prophylactic vaccines, and regular check-ups and immunization through yearly booster shots keep pet dogs in good health. With careful dietary management and good veterinary care even dogs with serious ailments such as cancer, and those with old-age problems, are able to lead a reasonably good life. The advanced diagnostic, surgical and therapeutic techniques available ensure quality veterinary health care for your dog.

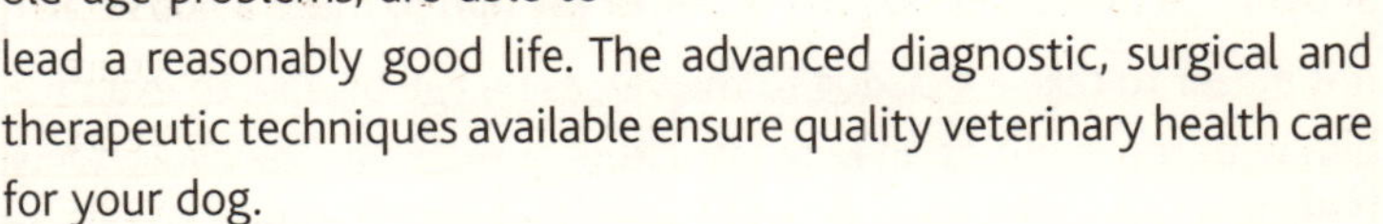

What should one consider while selecting a vet?

All small-animal practising veterinarians are graduates in veterinary science, and the degrees awarded by veterinary colleges in India are BVSc and AH. Some vets also have postgraduate qualifications in clinical subjects, such as medicine and surgery, which is desirable for a practising vet. The most important consideration, however, should be a vet's experience and reputation. You are advised to visit his clinic, speak to him, note the cleanliness in the clinic, and inquire about the facilities available. Vets who have had special training abroad score over others, as in India very few veterinary colleges offer special training in canine practice. Discuss health problems your dog may have had with the vet, and judge his response. Ask him about the emergency services offered by the clinic, the standby arrangements in case he goes on leave/falls sick, his professional fees, and also his charges for common procedures such as spaying and neutering. The proximity of the vet's clinic to your home is another major consideration. Developing a personal rapport with your dog's vet is also of utmost importance.

Should one go to the same vet every time?

To provide continuity of treatment it is better to have a regular vet. For vaccinations and annual health check-ups, it does not really matter if you visit someone else. Normally, however, most people like to have a regular vet, as he is familiar with the dog's medical history and has a record of his previous ailments.

Should one take a sick dog to the vet, or ask him to make a house call?

It is better to take a sick dog to the vet, as he will be able to examine him with the facilities and infrastructure available at the clinic. Only if the dog is very sick and old, and the clinic closed, should you request your vet to make a house call.

Health Parameters—Signs of Good Health and Sickness

As a dog owner you should be familiar with some of the normal health parameters of a dog. This will help you identify illness at an early stage, so that urgent remedial action can be taken.

A healthy dog is robust, alert and high-spirited; he loves play,

exercise and close contact with humans. Once you understand his daily routine and behaviour, assessing your dog's health will soon become natural. Any deviation from the norm will be immediately obvious.

Dogs have a finely-tuned biological clock. Therefore, if your dog does not get up at his usual time, is reluctant to play, eats less, behaves in an abnormal way, or you notice any change in the colour, consistency or quantity of his faeces, it is an indication that he is sick, and you should contact your vet immediately.

Some Important Health Parameters For a Dog

Health Parameters	Normal Values	
Body temperature	101.5°F-102°F (rectal), 38.5°C-38.9°C	
Respiration (resting)	Young dogs	20-28 per minute
	Old dogs	15-22 per minute
Pulse rate	Young dogs (femoral pulse, inner thigh)	110-130 per minute
	Adult large breeds Adult small breeds	80-100 per minute 100-120 per minute

How do you know if your dog is sick?

A sick dog is dull and depressed and does not take interest in his normal routine activities. He is much less energetic than usual and often suffers from loss of appetite. He wants to lie down/sleep quietly on his bed, or hide under his owner's bed; he does not drink water, or has more than usual; he vomits or has loose motions.

Is it true that the nose of a healthy dog is wet?

Fluid secreted by the lateral glands in a dog's nose keeps it moist. A moist, cool nose is generally considered a sign of good health in a dog. However, this is not always true, especially if the dog has been sleeping in a hot place, or has had distemper in his early life. A dog that has suffered from distemper has a dry nose, because the disease permanently damages the nasal glands.

How do you take a dog's temperature?

Either put a muzzle on him, or have someone hold him from the front. Insert a normal thermometer (about one inch) into the dog's anus, after lubricating the bulb with Vaseline (petroleum jelly). Keep it in place for about a minute, take it out, and after cleaning it with a piece of cotton wool, read the temperature.

How do you locate your dog's pulse?

The femoral artery, which is located on the inside of the thigh of the hind leg, is usually preferred for reading the pulse of a dog.

How is the respiration of a sick dog recorded?

Respiration is counted either by observing the rise and fall of chest movements of the dog or by putting the back of the hand in front of the dog's nose and counting the expiratory flow of air from the lungs as it strikes the hand.

Immunization and Preventive Health Care

Protection against contagious/infectious canine diseases caused by bacteria and viruses is either passive or active. Passive immunization is short-lived and is passed on by the mother dog to her puppies, whereas the dog acquires active immunization, which is long-lasting, by means of a vaccination schedule. However, to maintain protective antibodies at an optimum level, annual booster shots are given to adult dogs throughout their lives. Diseases such as rabies, distemper, hepatitis, leptospirosis, parvovirus and corona virus are very dangerous

and often fatal. In fact rabies is fatal for dogs as well as humans. Therefore, you must protect your dog from these deadly diseases with the aid of preventive health care.

The benefits of a preventive health care programme are many—it will lengthen and enhance the quality of your dog's life; your pet will have greater vitality and fewer health problems, and look good too. It will also ensure that canine health problems are not transmitted to human beings. Therefore, not only is preventive health care a wise investment, but it also costs substantially less than treatment!

Passive Immunity

A puppy acquires passive immunity from its mother in her womb, and also through colostrum, which is rich in passive antibodies. By providing this unique protection, nature equips the puppy with ammunition to face infections present in the environment. Without it, he would not be able to survive. This passive immunity, however, only provides protection against diseases for twelve to fourteen weeks. The negative aspect of maternal immunity is that it interferes with the active immunization acquired through vaccination.

Active Immunity

Protect your puppy from contagious/infectious diseases through active immunization by a series of vaccinations, starting at the age of six to seven weeks. Immunity through vaccinations provides protection for a much longer duration compared to the passive immunity acquired from the mother dog. However, annual booster vaccinations are necessary for providing lifelong protection to dogs.

Why is sucking colostrum during the first twenty-four hours of a puppy's birth so important for its survival?

The antibodies contained in colostrum can pass through the puppy's intestines only for a limited period of time. Since these antibodies provide passive protection for the puppy, it is important that he sucks an adequate quantity of milk during the first twenty-four hours of his life.

Does the mother provide uniform passive protection to all her puppies?

No, this depends on the colostrum intake of each puppy. Puppies that have more colostrum acquire a higher level of passive immunity.

How long does this passive immunity protect puppies against diseases?

The duration of the protection provided by maternal antibodies varies widely. It could be as little as six to eight weeks or even less, or could extend from fourteen to eighteen weeks.

Is it possible to measure the levels of passive immunity?

Yes, it is, by means of elaborate laboratory tests, the facilities for which normally do not exist even in well-equipped diagnostic laboratories.

Why should one start active immunization so early in the life of a puppy?

Since it is not possible to assess the level of passive protection provided by the mother, it is essential to administer the first shots at the age of six to seven weeks. Otherwise the puppy will be without any protection, and may contract serious contagious diseases.

What is the vaccination schedule for puppies and adult dogs?

The vaccination schedule for puppies and adult dogs is as follows:

Age	Vaccine
6 to 7 weeks	DHLPP (combined distemper, hepatitis, leptospirosis, para-influenza and parvovirus) vaccine
8 weeks	Corona virus vaccine
11 to 12 weeks	DHLPP (first booster)
13 weeks	Corona virus (first booster)
14 weeks	Rabies (killed virus vaccine)
16 weeks	DHLPP (second booster)
17 weeks	Corona virus (second booster)
20 to 22 weeks	Parvovirus (third booster)
9 months	Rabies (first booster)
1 year 3 months	Annual booster for DHLPP + Corona virus
1 year 9 months	Annual booster for Rabies
N.B.: Annual booster shots for DHLPP + Corona + Rabies should be administered throughout the dog's life.	

Why are the first and second boosters for DHLPP and the third booster for parvovirus administered to puppies?

Since the passive immunity from maternal antibodies interferes with the development of active immunity (through vaccines), multiple booster injections are required to ensure the development of protective active immunity. As long as the maternal antibodies are present in puppies (which may be until the age of eighteen to twenty weeks as in the case of Parvovirus), they react with the antigen contained in the vaccines and neutralize it. As a result of this active antibodies are not formed. That is why the third booster for parvovirus is given when the puppies are twenty to twenty-two weeks old.

What precautions should be taken to ensure that the vaccines provide adequate protection?

Puppies/adult dogs should be in healthy condition when they are vaccinated, and they should have been dewormed at least a week earlier. Only disposable syringes should be used, and the vaccine should have been properly stored in a refrigerator and not expired. Do not expose the puppies/dogs to any kind of infection for a month after they have been vaccinated.

How long does it take puppies or dogs to develop active antibodies after they have been vaccinated?

Normally it takes three to four weeks for the vaccines to develop sufficient levels of antibodies in vaccinated puppies or dogs. However, very weak and debilitated animals may not respond positively to vaccination. Diseases/parasites in vaccinated dogs interfere with the development of antibodies.

Can one be a hundred per cent certain that administration of the recommended vaccines will provide foolproof protection to the dog?

Adequate protection is provided by vaccination in ninety per cent of healthy puppies and dogs. However, there cannot be a hundred per cent guarantee of total protection, failures can occur due to a number of reasons.

Administration of Medicines and Bandaging

As a dog owner you must have a working knowledge of veterinary first aid, which includes the administration of tablets and liquid medicines, and bandaging. Most vets prescribe the administration of oral medicines at home as follow-up treatment.

Pet dogs may need emergency treatment and bandaging of

bleeding wounds and injuries. Therefore, you should know how to bandage a wound, as first-aid treatment.

What is the correct method of administering a tablet/capsule to a dog?

ADMINISTERING TABLET

The dog must first be made to sit down. Holding him firmly with your knees while you are standing over him, open his mouth by pulling the upper jaw upwards, and press just behind the canine teeth with your left hand. Take the capsule/tablet in your right hand (between the thumb and index finger), and open and push the lower jaw down with the remaining fingers of your right hand. The dog's mouth is fully open now. Place the tablet/capsule as far back on the tongue as possible and close the mouth quickly. Keeping the mouth closed with your left hand, raise the chin and rub the throat gently with the right hand, to help the dog swallow the tablet/capsule. Praise him after he has swallowed it. Dry pills/capsules can be greased with vegetable oil.

Is there an easier way of administering a tablet to a dog?

Hide the tablet/capsule in a small piece of the dog's favourite food, such as meat or cheese; or sandwiched between a piece of bread. You can also conceal it in a chicken's heart and feed it to the dog. Alternatively, crush a tablet and mix it with sugar and water. This can be administered to the dog in a syringe.

What is the best method of administering liquid medicine?

Draw the liquid medicine into a plastic syringe (without a needle). Make the dog sit down. Insert the syringe into his mouth from the side, near the angle of the mouth, and slowly inject the medicine; the dog will swallow it. Or make a pouch by drawing up the corners of the dog's mouth on one side, and then gradually push in the medicine (through a syringe) into this pouch. (The dog's mouth should be pointed upwards so that the medicine does not come out.) Stop immediately if the dog starts coughing. This happens if the medicine goes down the windpipe.

What is the most reliable method of administering medicines to dogs?

Injections are the most reliable method.

What is the best way of administering eardrops to a dog?

Dogs often suffer from ear infection, and as follow-up treatment, you will have to administer eardrops at home. The following is the recommended procedure:

- Make the dog sit and put a muzzle on him.
- Lift the flap of the ear; clean any visible wax with cotton wool dampened with warm water.
- Hold the dog's head with your left hand, and the ear drops in your right hand.
- Invert the eardrop dispenser over the inside of the dog's ear and squeeze the appropriate number of drops into the ear.
- Without letting the dog shake his head, let the earflap fall back into its normal position, and gently massage the ear with the palm of your right hand.

How are eye drops administered to a dog?

Dogs often contract eye infections, leading to discharge from the eyes and accumulation of mucous. The following is the recommended procedure for administering eye drops:

- Make the dog sit and muzzle him.
- Clean the eyes gently with moistened cotton wool.
- Hold the muzzle with your left hand to control the dog's head.
- With the right hand, hold the inverted bottle of eye drops and gently squeeze the required number of drops into the eye or eyes.

How is eye ointment applied to a dog's eyes?

After cleaning the dog's eye with moistened cotton wool, apply the eye ointment inside his lower eyelid, making sure the nozzle of the tube does not touch the eye. Gently hold the eye closed for a few seconds while the ointment spreads inside. The dog should be in a sitting position and muzzled.

When should the anal glands of a dog be cleaned?

Dogs with packed anal glands drag their hindquarters on the ground and lick the anal area, trying to relieve the pressure. To empty the anal glands, wear rubber gloves and keep some cotton wool in your hand. Using the thumb and forefinger, hold a tissue on either side of the anus and gently squeeze it. Foul-smelling secretions will spurt out like a jet. Clean the area properly after the glands have been emptied. This requires skill and practice and you may have to take the help of a vet to do it correctly.

How do you bandage a cut on a dog's paw to stop the bleeding?

After cleaning the bleeding paw with running tap water, apply a sterilized gauze pad that has been soaked in cold water on the wound and hold it firmly against the paw. Minor bleeding will stop with digital pressure on the gauze pad. To prevent the bleeding from starting again, secure the pad with a bandage. After first aid has been administered, take the dog to a vet for treatment. Severe arterial bleeding may require constant digital pressure on the gauze pad until a vet ligates the bleeding vessel.

How would you bandage a cut wound on a dog's ear?

Dogs often get cuts and tears on their ears in dog fights. The ears bleed profusely and require immediate attention. Calm your dog by reassuring him, clean the wound with liquid Betadine, and apply a sterilized gauze pad over it. Then wrap the ear with a bandage around the head to prevent it from bleeding again, especially when the dog shakes his head. Make sure the bandage is not too tight and is not exerting pressure on the windpipe. Take the dog to the vet to get the wound treated and bandaged properly.

How do you bandage a tail wound?

Dogs get tail injuries, as their tails often get caught in closing doors. Tails also bleed profusely, and wagging further compounds this. After cleaning the damaged area with a sterilized gauze pad soaked in cold water, apply Betadine liquid, cover it with another gauze pad, and bandage it. As the bleeding can start again when the dog wags his tail, it is advisable to bandage it right down to the level of the umbilicus, to prevent him from wagging it. Make sure the bandage is not too tight, and take the dog to the vet for proper treatment.

How is a cut on a dog's abdomen bandaged?

First clean the wound with plenty of water, apply liquid Betadine, and then a sterilized gauze pad, and bandage it with a towel or pillow cover. Take your dog to the vet for further treatment.

Can one use a cotton wool pad if a gauze pad is not available?

You should not use cotton wool directly on a cut as cotton fibres get into the wound and are difficult to remove later. If a gauze pad is

not available, make a pad with a bandage and use it instead of cotton wool.

Common Health Problems and Remedies

There are some common health problems dogs suffer from, and it is essential for you to understand the symptoms and administer veterinary first aid at home in an emergency. Remember that first aid is not a substitute for veterinary treatment; your pet must be taken to the vet after administering first aid because some common symptoms such as vomiting can be life-threatening and should not be taken lightly. Only a vet can treat a sick dog properly. In fact, before administering any first aid in an emergency at home, consult your vet first on the telephone, and follow it up by taking your dog to him as soon as possible. Unlike human beings, dogs cannot speak about their health problems, so it is a challenging task even for a vet to arrive at a correct diagnosis. However, having armed yourself with basic knowledge about common health problems, you will be in a better position to explain the problem to your vet, and also to deal with an emergency.

Digestive Problems

Dogs have a tendency to overeat whenever food is freely available to them. Hence they are more prone to vomiting, diarrhoea and constipation. They have large stomachs and relatively small intestines therefore they can survive on a single large meal on a daily basis.

What are the causes of vomiting and what should I do if my dog vomits?

Vomiting is a common problem in dogs and can be caused by overeating, intestinal worms, gastroenteritis, eating garbage/grass, travel sickness, and many other reasons. It is also a symptom of several serious infectious diseases, such as parvovirus, corona virus, hepatitis, urino-genital-tract infections, ear infections, brain tumours, or some electrolyte imbalance. Allow your dog to rest and do not give him solid food for at least twelve hours. Give him small quantities of water every few hours. Depending on the size of the dog, administer half to one tablet of Perinorm, as first aid. If vomiting persists, consult your vet immediately, as it can cause severe dehydration, which can be life-threatening. If the vomit is bloodstained or chocolate coloured, it is a very serious problem, which could be a symptom of parvovirus or gastric torsion. Immediate help should be sought in such cases.

What are the common causes of diarrhoea in dogs? How should one administer first aid at home for this problem?

Worm infestation, scavenging, poisoning, overeating, gastroenteritis, infectious diseases (such as parvovirus, corona virus, hepatitis), pancreatitis, emotional upsets or food allergy can cause diarrhoea. The dog goes off his food and becomes dull and depressed; there is a tendency to drink excessive water. Some dogs get diarrhoea due to lactic (milk) intolerance. While food should be withheld for twelve to twenty-four hours, the dog must have access to water. The treatment depends on the cause, but in simple diarrhoea, bland food such as rice and chicken soup can be given in small quantities several times a day. Diarrhoea mixed with blood is a serious condition and you should

consult your vet immediately. Depending on the size of the dog, administer half to one tablet of Dependal-M or Furoxone Suspension (one to two teaspoons) orally two or three times a day to control simple diarrhoea.

Why do dogs get constipated? How can one help a constipated dog?

Constipation in dogs can be caused by consumption of too much meat and bones. A constipated dog should be given more vegetables in his diet. Lack of exercise and fibre in the food, de-hydration and general debility can also lead to this problem. A constipated dog strains while defecating, and the faeces are hard and dry. To prevent constipation, exercise your dog regularly and include adequate fibre in his diet. As a home remedy give him 10-20 ml liquid paraffin at night. If the constipation persists, consult the vet.

What causes loss of appetite in a dog?

Loss of appetite could be due to many reasons such as digestive disorders, fever caused by contagious/infectious diseases, discomfort in the mouth/teeth, or anxiety. It is often the first sign of illness in a dog. Consult the vet about the seriousness of the dog's condition and find out the exact cause of the problem.

Fever

Fever is an elevation of the body temperature above the normal range and is often the first symptom of illness. It is the protective reaction of the body, and is usually the result of invasion by bacteria/viruses. It can be caused by environmental factors such as heat, sometimes resulting in heatstroke. Excessive exercise in hot weather can also cause fever.

What are the symptoms of fever in a dog? How does one treat them?

Fever is a symptom of serious illness, and could be caused by several factors. There is a rise in the body temperature; the dog becomes dull and depressed, and goes off his food. All contagious/infectious diseases start with fever, so if your dog is running a temperature, administer Paracetamol syrup/tablet to him at home after consulting your vet about the problem. If the fever is very high, ice/cold packs may have to be applied on the dog's head, to bring down the temperature.

Respiratory Problems

Generally, dogs do not suffer much from respiratory problems. Coughing is a common problem, and can be caused by bacterial infection or heart disease in older dogs. Certain bacterial and viral diseases, such as canine distemper, can also result in respiratory problems, which can also give rise to abnormal/laboured breathing, snoring, sneezing and voice changes in dogs.

What is the cause of kennel cough in dogs?

Kennel cough is a bacterial disease that is highly contagious and causes inflammation of the larynx (voice box) and trachea. A dog suffering from kennel cough makes a peculiar sound while coughing. He should be kept segregated from other dogs. Kennel cough is a serious condition, and veterinary help should immediately be sought.

Why does a dog sometimes sneeze constantly?

On waking up almost all dogs sneeze, but constant sneezing could be due to an allergy or infection. There is no discharge in allergic sneezing, but sneezing due to bacterial/viral infections is accompanied with purulent or bloody discharge. Tumours/foreign bodies in the nostril can also cause sneezing. Only a vet, after a thorough examination, can diagnose the exact cause of constant sneezing, and prescribe the correct treatment.

What could be the cause of a persistent cough, which occurs only at night, in an old dog?

Persistent nighttime coughing in older dogs is a symptom of a cardiac condition. It is generally a non-productive cough and also occurs after exercise. Older dogs sometimes suffer from chronic bronchitis, which could also cause a persistent cough. One should consult the vet as soon as possible, as this kind of cough is invariably a symptom of a serious disease and needs proper diagnosis and treatment.

Why do some dogs snore?

Snoring could be due to several reasons, but it is commonly observed in breeds with compressed faces, such as Boxers, Pugs and Pekingese. Their soft palates are heavy and hang at the back of their throats. This interferes with the larynx and produces a snore. Older dogs often snore. Allergic inflammation of the throat can also cause snoring. Only a vet can treat this problem.

What are the causes of breathing abnormalities in dogs? Are they serious in nature?

Distressed breathing is the sign of a potentially life-threatening problem. It is observed in cases of pleural infusions, injury to the rib cage, serious lung disease, heart failure, kidney disease, heat stroke and poisoning. Immediate veterinary help should be sought for this condition.

Do dogs suffer from bronchitis and pneumonia?

Yes, dogs do suffer from bronchitis and pneumonia, especially from exposure to cold weather, and it can be acute or chronic. Bacteria such as tuberculosis bacilli, and certain viruses such as distemper virus, are generally responsible for bronchitis in dogs. If it is not treated in time, it can result in pneumonia. The most common symptom in bronchitis is constant coughing accompanied by fever, discharge from the nostrils, respiratory distress and loss of appetite. It is a serious condition, which requires immediate treatment with antibiotics prescribed by the vet. The dog must be kept warm, away from draughts, and should be given a light, nourishing diet, such as chicken soup.

What is the cause of bleeding from the nose in dogs? What does one do if this happens?

Bleeding from the nose in dogs can occur due to several reasons such as mechanical injury, inflammatory lesions in the nasal bones/mucous membranes, or a tumour/growth in the nasal passage. It can also be caused by a tick-borne protozoan infection called ehrlichiosis. As first aid, place ice cubes or a towel soaked in cold water on the dog's head. Take him to the vet for thorough diagnosis and treatment, as soon as possible.

Internal Parasites

All dogs suffer from intestinal parasites such as roundworms, tapeworms, hookworms and threadworms. They are also infected by protozoan parasites such as coccidia and giardia. These are not only harmful for dogs, but are a potential health hazard for human beings too. Regular deworming of dogs is therefore essential. Dogs infested with worms generally have an increased appetite, which may be accompanied by eating grass/garbage, vomiting, and diarrhoea. Such dogs also often suffer from skin problems, and have a rough coat and a potbelly. Sometimes one can see the worms in the faeces of an infected dog. The dog licks its anus, and the area under the tail becomes red. Convulsions and fits may occur in a heavily infested dog. Dogs can also be affected by heartworms, which are common in the USA. Incidences of heartworm infestation have also been reported in the north-eastern states of India.

Do puppies and adult dogs have the same kind of intestinal worms?

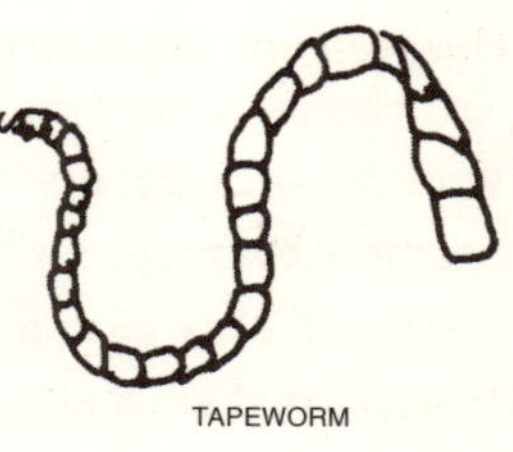

TAPEWORM

Almost all puppies suffer from roundworm infection, which is acquired either before birth or through their mother's milk after they are born. Adult dogs generally suffer from all types of worms.

How can one make out the difference between a roundworm, a hookworm and a tapeworm?

One can see roundworms with the naked eye; they look like pale earthworms and are about eight to ten centimetres in length. On the other hand, tapeworms are flat and segmented parasites that are generally passed out as individual segments, and look like rice grains. Tapeworm segments can be seen in fresh dog faeces (they curl up and move about) they are also sometimes seen sticking to the infested dog's fur in the anal region. Hookworms are very fine thread-like worms, hardly a centimetre long, and are difficult to identify, unlike roundworms and tapeworms.

How do human beings contract worm infection from dogs?

Roundworms and hookworms (from dogs) can infect human beings by accidentally ingesting the eggs of these worms. Hookworm larvae can penetrate the human skin. Infected dogs shed the eggs of worms in their faeces. Children playing on contaminated ground, or with infected dogs, are most likely to contract these infections. You must, therefore, always wash your hands before eating, especially after grooming your dog or playing with him. Children should not be allowed to play in an area where dogs defecate. If the dog has defecated in the house, the faeces should be immediately disposed off properly and the area disinfected.

How can one avoid contracting worm infections from dogs?

You can prevent human infestation by keeping pet dogs free from worms. Since puppies get infected with roundworms from their mothers even before they are born, and the infection is further reinforced after birth by infection through milk, it is very important to deworm them and their mother when they are three to four weeks old. After that the puppies should be dewormed according to the advice of the vet, every fortnight, till they are three months old. Deworming should be done at monthly intervals thereafter till the puppies are six months old. Subsequently, it should be done every three months, with periodic stool-sample check-ups.

How can one prevent puppies from being infected by their mother?

Before breeding, the female dog should be dewormed according to the advice of your vet. If it is not possible to do so before mating, she should be dewormed within the first week of breeding or after three to four weeks of mating. Otherwise, if a pregnant dog is infested with roundworms, she will definitely pass on the infection to her puppies before they are even born.

How do roundworms damage the health of puppies/adult dogs?

Roundworms thrive on the dog's food (in its stomach and small intestine). In puppies, they can cause a fatal intestinal obstruction, or even rupture the intestines when present in large numbers. They do not, however, suck blood. In adult dogs, roundworms do not cause severe damage, unless the infestation is very heavy. Infected puppies have distended abdomens and often suffer from vomiting; sometimes the worms are vomited out by the infected dog or puppy.

How do adult dogs get infected by roundworms?

Ingesting the eggs through contaminated food or water infects adult

dogs. The eggs are passed out through the faeces, and sometimes stick to the fur on the hindquarters of infected dogs. If another adult dog or puppy licks the contaminated fur on the dog's hindquarters, he can get infected. Therefore, this infection is very easily spread. Dogs can also contract worm infestation by walking on infected ground. After the dog has ingested the eggs, they develop into larvae in the dog's stomach/intestine, from where they enter the bloodstream, and finally reach the lungs. They are coughed up from the lungs and swallowed again into the stomach/intestine, where they mature into adult worms and start producing eggs that are passed out with the faeces, thus completing their life cycle.

How do dogs get infected by hookworms?

Like roundworms, puppies can contract hookworm infection when they are still in the womb. Puppies and adult dogs are also infected through food and water contaminated with the larvae of these worms. Hookworm infection can also occur due to larvae penetrating the skin.

How do hookworms harm dogs?

Hookworms are bloodsucking parasites and cause severe anemia and blood loss. Infected puppies and dogs become emaciated and anaemic. These worms also cause severe damage and ulceration in the walls of the intestines. Heavy hookworm infection can be fatal if not treated in time.

How is a hookworm infection detected?

The best way to detect a hookworm infection is by a microscopic examination of the dog's faeces.

How do tapeworms infect dogs?

One kind of tapeworm infects dogs when the dog eats dog fleas containing tapeworm eggs. Infection from other types of tapeworms is contracted by eating the offal/carcasses of animals such as sheep, which contain cysts produced by tapeworm eggs.

How do giardia/coccidia infections harm dogs?

These microscopic protozoan parasites infect dogs when they drink contaminated water, causing diarrhoea, especially in young dogs. This can be accompanied by mucous and blood. Microscopic examination of the faeces is necessary for a diagnosis of the infection. Your vet will be able to treat these infections after a confirmed diagnosis.

Common Skin Disorders

Skin disorders are the commonest health problems observed in dogs. Dogs with skin problems constantly lick and scratch themselves, which results in hair loss and damage to the skin. This, in turn, results in inflammation due to bacterial or fungal infection. Proper daily grooming of the dog can help in preventing skin disorders, through early detection and timely treatment. Skin disorders are classified depending on the cause, that is, eczema/dermatitis, urticaria, allergic reactions, ringworms and mange/scabies. They do not pose any danger to the dog's life, but are the cause of incessant itching, irritation and scratching. Skin disorders are generally slow to heal, and take a long time to get completely cured.

What is eczema/dermatitis? How does one prevent it in dogs?

Eczema/dermatitis is a general term used for inflammation of the skin. It is characterized by redness and itching, and can be acute or chronic, dry or wet, with oozing sores. Generally, it is of fungal origin, and bacteria may be the secondary invaders. Due to constant scratching, the skin thickens and circular patches with irregular borders appear on the skin. There is hair loss in the affected area. Eczema/

dermatitis can also be caused by allergy from food/drugs or internal parasites (worms). Regular grooming and deworming help in preventing this disorder. This is a serious problem, which should not be neglected, and veterinary help should be taken at the initial stages of the disease.

What is urticaria?

The term urticaria is used to describe skin eruptions that appear suddenly, either due to drug allergy or insect bites. Antihistamines such as Avil/Phenergan, administered by an injection or orally, help in relieving the symptoms of urticaria. Sometimes urticarial eruptions can also appear due to food allergy. A dog afflicted with urticaria is restless and scratches himself all the time. Consult your vet regarding the proper treatment.

What is a ringworm infection? How can one prevent one's dog from being infected by it?

This is a fungal infection that attacks the hair and skin. A ring-like red patch appears on the skin, and there is loss of hair in the affected area. The outer part of the ring is highly infectious, and owners are at risk of infection through their dogs. Therefore, you should wash your hands properly after handling an infected dog. The external application of anti-fungal ointments/powders, combined with good hygiene, helps in overcoming the infection. However, consult your vet regarding the right treatment for ringworm infection.

What is mange/scabies? How do dogs get infected with it?

Mange/scabies is a serious skin disease commonly found in dogs. It is caused by small mange mites, which cannot be seen by the naked eye. There are two main types of mange mites that attack dogs: sarcoptic mange mites and demodex mange mites. Poor hygienic conditions, lack of proper nutrition, poor immune status, heavy worm infestation, and lack of proper grooming are some predisposing factors for mange.

What are the special features of sarcoptic mange?

Sarcoptic mange mites burrow into the skin, especially at the tips of the ears and the elbows, and cause intense irritation and itching. Later the disease spreads all over the body: the back, armpits and inner sides of the thighs. Dogs of all ages can be affected, but it is more common in puppies and young dogs. The disease is acquired by direct contact with an infected animal or contaminated clothing, and the diagnosis is confirmed by a microscopic examination of the skin scrapings from the affected area. Children and adult human beings are at risk by dogs suffering from sarcoptic mange.

What are the special features of demodex mange?

Demodex mange mites normally live on the skin of all dogs. However, when the resistance of the dog is low due to malnutrition or a heavy worm infestation, they multiply and attack the hair follicles. This causes a disease called red mange, which is heritable and generally passed on from an infected mother to her puppies. It usually starts from the head, around the eyes, muzzle, tips of the ears and forelegs. The affected skin reddens and the dog's hair starts falling. Short-haired dogs such as Boxers and Dachshunds are more prone to demodex mange. The dogs develop pustules in the affected area, as a result of secondary bacterial infection, and exude a mousy odour from their bodies. The mites invade the lymphatic system in the skin, which becomes thick and wrinkled. The diagnosis is confirmed by a microscopic examination of the skin

MANGE PARASITE

scrapings from the affected area. Red mange is a very serious skin disease and needs to be treated under the guidance of a vet, with weekly insecticide baths. It takes a long time to get cured. This disease is common in stray dogs.

How does one prevent the transmission of demodex mange from a mother dog to her puppies?

A predisposition to demodex mange is genetically linked, and an affected mother, who has inherited it herself, passes this on to puppies. In order to prevent this, female puppies suffering from red mange should be spayed so that the infection ends with them.

Why do some dogs keep licking themselves, especially on the limbs, causing chronic ulcers?

Dogs normally lick their skins to clean their fur. Excessive licking of certain parts could be due to a psychological disorder which causes lick dermatitis/lick granuloma. Obsessive licking is difficult to control without proper medication by a vet. However, lack of proper exercise and boredom can also be responsible for excessive/obsessive licking.

Can hormonal imbalance in dogs lead to hair loss and skin problems?

Generalized symmetrical hair loss is of hormonal origin. The thyroid, adrenal and pituitary glands, or the testes/ovaries are generally responsible for causing hormonal imbalance. Proper investigation by a vet can help in pinpointing the cause and the treatment.

Why do most dogs suffer from hair loss on their elbows on both sides of the front legs?

Hair loss on the elbows is more pronounced in bigger/heavier dogs, and is caused by excessive pressure being exerted on them when lying down on a hard surface. This results in callus formation and hair loss. Application of a skin cream/Vaseline on the elbows will keep the skin supple and prevent the formation of calluses. The dog should also be provided with soft bedding; this will help in preventing hair loss.

Are older dogs more prone to skin and hair-coat disorders?

Ageing causes certain changes in the skin and hair coat, making it more susceptible to skin diseases. A general thinning of the hair coat takes place in older dogs and their skin becomes drier, or sometimes greasier, due to changes in the sebaceous (oil-producing) glands. These glands may develop nodules called sebaceous cysts. In the same way as the susceptibility of dogs to ticks and fleas increases with age, skin disorders due to hormonal changes are more common in older dogs; chronic illness and diabetes also causes skin problems, and stress is considered a contributory factor.

Many dogs suffer from dry skin and dandruff. What causes this condition, and how can one prevent it?

Dry skin can be caused by excessive bathing or changes in the sebaceous glands. Affected dogs should be bathed at monthly intervals with a light shampoo containing selenium. They should be regularly groomed and given Omega-3 fatty acids in their diet. Adding oil (any cooking oil) to the food of affected dogs helps in improving their skin. Cod liver oil is very good for getting rid of dandruff.

What shampoo should one use for crusting and itchy skin conditions in dogs?

Dogs suffering from bacterial skin infections/allergies/seborrhoea and excessively oily skin should be bathed with keratolytic agents, to remove skin debris. Sulphur tar shampoos containing coal tar and salicylic acid are the best remedies for this condition.

Ear Problems

Dogs often suffer from ear problems. Those with pendulous and long ears, such as Cocker Spaniels, have more ear problems than breeds with erect ears. The first sign of any ear disorder is the dog shaking his head and scratching his ear. A foul-smelling discharge, and the dog's head tilting to the side of the diseased ear follow this. Deafness is common in elderly dogs. Some dogs suffer from loss of balance due to ear disorders. Haematoma of the earflap is another common disorder in dogs.

EAR CLEANING

Why do dogs often shake their heads and scratch their ears?

This is generally due to an infection, or the presence of ear mites in the ear. Excessive wax in the ears, an allergy or a foreign body, can also cause this condition. You should consult a vet as soon as possible; he will examine the ear and let you know the exact cause and treatment for this problem.

What is earflap haematoma and how is it caused?

Earflap haematoma is an accumulation of blood caused by a rupture of blood vessels in the earflap. A dog suffering from an infection/irritation in the ear violently shakes his head, and this leads to the rupturing of the blood vessels. The swelling, caused by haematoma, can be as big as an egg. It is an extremely painful condition, which needs the immediate surgical intervention of a vet, who will drain the haematoma, stitch the ear and bandage it to the head.

How can ear problems in dogs be prevented?

The ears should be periodically checked and cleaned by a vet to remove any excessive wax/foreign body. The owner should also clean the insides of the earflaps gently with wet cotton wool during daily grooming. The cleaning of the internal ear should, however, be left to the vet. Older dogs need to get their ears cleaned more often than younger ones.

Why is deafness associated with white-coloured dogs?

This is due to a genetic defect in the inner ear, which is linked to a white coat/colour, and predisposes them to deafness. The problem is common in white Boxers, Bull Terriers and Dalmatians.

What causes discharge from the ears in dogs and how does one tackle this problem?

Discharge from the ears is due to a bacterial or fungal infection which causes inflammation of the ear, and is known as otitis. It can also be caused by ear mites, and is a serious and painful condition which needs treatment with antibiotics and anti-inflammatory drugs prescribed by a vet. A chronic case of otitis is known as canker of the ear, which may need surgery and is difficult to treat.

Eye Problems

Dogs often suffer from eye problems such as conjunctivitis, opacity of the cornea, cataract, and traumatic injuries leading to prolapse of the eyeball. Older dogs suffer from loss of vision caused by progressive degenerative changes related to ageing. Discharge from the eyes is also a very common problem. In order to relieve the irritation, the dog may hurt his eye by scratching with his paws. Breeds with bulging

eyes, such as Pekingese and Pugs, sometimes accidentally damage their eyes. Eye problems are easy to detect and the owner should not neglect them.

What causes discharge from a dog's eyes, and what can one do about it?

Infection, irritation or a foreign body in the eye causes it to emit a discharge. It can also be due to an allergic condition. In normal circumstances, the tear duct drains the tears at the back of the nose, but the mucous produced from infection blocks the tear ducts, and discharge from the eyes begins to flow. Constant eye discharge stains the dog's face brown. If your pet suffers from this problem, consult your vet immediately, as this condition may need the tear duct to be de-clogged and treated with antibiotic/anti-allergic eye drops.

What is the cause of conjunctivitis? What should one do if one's dog contracts it?

Conjunctivitis is an inflammation of the conjunctival membranes and is a very common problem in dogs. It may be a symptom of distemper. Dust/foreign bodies can cause conjunctivitis too. The symptoms of conjunctivitis are redness, swelling of the eyes with excessive discharge, and a tendency on the part of the dog to keep his eyelids closed. Veterinary treatment should be sought immediately, but as a first-aid measure you should clean the discharge with moist cotton wool.

What is the difference between opacity of the cornea and cataract?

Opacity of the cornea is either caused by corneal injury or the retention of fluid in the cornea (outermost layer of the eyeball), caused by certain diseases. The eye may look bluish-gray in colour. Cataract is a much more serious problem and is caused by the lens becoming opaque; this is common in old dogs. Cataract develops gradually and may need surgical removal in totally blind dogs. Corneal injuries need immediate veterinary help.

Sometimes, due to dogfights or trauma, there is a prolapsed eyeball. What should one do in such a situation?

Prolapsed eyeball is a condition where the eyeball is pushed out of its socket. It is a serious condition that requires treatment from a vet. The dog should be taken for emergency treatment immediately. Any loss of time can damage the eye, resulting in loss of vision.

Urinary Tract Problems

Urinary Tract Infections (UTI) are fairly common in elderly dogs. Difficulty in passing urine or straining to urinate can be caused by an infection or might be due to urinary calculi (stones). Blood in the urine (haematuria) is sometimes observed in dogs with severe UTI, urinary calculi, or in certain infectious or contagious diseases. A sudden increase/decrease in the quantity of urine is also a serious metabolic illness associated with diseases such as diabetes or hormonal imbalance.

What is the cause of increased urination in dogs?

Increased urination in dogs is generally due to kidney or urinary tract infections, common in older dogs. Diabetes and certain liver diseases cause increased urine formation, but this may also be due to an excessive intake of water. Dogs being treated with corticosteroids also produce excessive urine. In such cases, a sample of the dog's urine should be collected and examined in a pathological laboratory or veterinary clinic, to find out the exact cause.

What is the cause of decreased urination in dogs?

Decreased urination is the result of dehydration/fever/sickness in a dog, and the urine is dark yellow in colour. This can also happen in the last stages of kidney failure. It is a serious condition, which needs urgent veterinary help. Dehydration is life-threatening and calls for immediate intravenous fluid therapy.

Sometimes dogs dribble urine. What causes this?

This condition often occurs in dogs that have injured their spinal cords, or suffer from hormonal imbalance. It is common in female dogs after they have been spayed. Chronic UTI and bladder displacement in old age may also cause dribbling/incontinence of urine. Veterinary help should be sought to help dogs suffering from this problem.

Why do some dogs strain while passing urine?

This could be due to several causes such as infection of the bladder/ urethral stones or enlargement of the prostrate gland in male dogs. The colour of the urine may be cloudy or tinged with blood. In male dogs, urethral stones sometimes get stuck behind the penis bone, causing severe straining and pain. The dog is unable to urinate and the bladder balloons up with accumulated urine. It is an emergency requiring immediate veterinary help.

Are urinary stones common in both sexes in dogs?

Elderly dogs of both sexes are predisposed to urinary calculi. A dog that is affected strains while passing urine, which may be mixed with blood. An X-ray of the lower abdomen reveals stones in the bladder or urethra. While bladder stones are common in both sexes, urethral stones generally occur in male dogs. Surgical removal is the only treatment for this condition. Consult your vet regarding appropriate treatment.

Nervous System Disorders

Injury, or certain bacterial/viral infections affecting the brain and spinal cord, can cause serious health problems in dogs. The common symptoms of nervous system disorders in dogs are lack of sensation; partial or complete paralysis; loss of balance; seizures/fits/convulsions; or behavioural changes. Viral infections such as distemper and rabies cause inflammation of the brain (encephalitis), which results in loss of balance, a change in temperament, seizures and death. Injuries to the spinal cord interfere with the transmission of nerve messages, and depending on their severity and the part of the cord involved, they may result in loss of sensation/paralysis of the hind legs, or urinary incontinence. Nervous system disorders are serious in nature and need immediate treatment by an experienced vet.

What is an epileptic fit or seizure, and what are the grand mal and petit mal syndromes in a dog?

A seizure or epileptic fit is a sudden loss of consciousness, and depending on its severity, it is classified as a grand mal seizure or petit mal episode. In a grand mal seizure, loss of consciousness is accompanied by salivation, twitching and violent convulsions/spasms, and the dog may also urinate and defecate. His whole body is affected, and he looks frightening. A petit mal seizure is less severe and dramatic and lasts for a few seconds, during which time the dog seems disoriented and may jerk his head. The severest of all seizures is known as status epilepticus, in which a series of seizures occur in quick succession. This can last for hours or days, and is invariably fatal. Traumatic/physical injury to the brain can result in fits, which also occur in a condition called eclampsia, when calcium

levels in the body drop drastically; or when blood sugar levels fall dangerously, especially in small or weak puppies stressed by sudden or long journeys.

What should one do when a dog is having seizures?

Try and protect the dog from injuring himself while he is having convulsions. Keep his air passage clear and make sure that his tongue is not blocking his throat. This should be done carefully so that you do not get bitten in the process. Make the dog comfortable, eliminate noise and reduce light. You must get immediate veterinary help for a dog having seizures. He should be put on anticonvulsant medicines; the dosage and duration of treatment varies with each case. Injecting calcium intravenously, or intravenous glucose injections in puppies with low blood sugar levels, treats eclampsia.

What happens when a dog has a stroke?

A stroke is the loss of function of a particular part of the body due to the brain cells being damaged, which is caused by the blood supply being cut off by a blood clot. Therefore, a stroke can affect any part of the body, causing paralysis. After a stroke a dog is unsure of himself, avoid foods and vomits. This is a serious ailment, which needs urgent veterinary help.

What is the cause of lack of coordination or paralysis of a dog's hind legs?

This condition is common in larger breeds such as German Shepherds and Great Danes, and is caused by a slipped disc and instability of the vertebrae, resulting in compression of the spinal cord. The affected dog is reluctant to jump or climb stairs. Serious damage to the spinal cord can cause paralysis of the hind legs and loss of bladder and bowel control.

What is the cause of behavioural changes in dogs?

Behavioural changes could be due to neurological causes. Rabies is the most serious disease in dogs, and causes marked change in their behaviour. Snapping at non-existent flies is a condition sometimes caused by psycho-motor problems, common in certain breeds such as King Charles' Spaniels. A dog exhibiting any kind of behavioural change must be taken to the vet for a veterinary examination and treatment, as this could be caused by a serious problem such as rabies.

Why do some dogs shake their facial and leg muscles uncontrollably?

Brain damage results in involuntary twitching of the facial and leg muscles, and is caused by the distemper virus. This condition is called chorea. It is incurable but anticonvulsant medicines may help relieve symptoms to a certain extent.

Bone and Joint Problems

The dog is a natural hunter and his agility and fitness depend on the condition of his musculo-skeletal system. The front legs of the dog bear sixty per cent of his body weight and they are attached to his body by muscles, as a dog does not have a collarbone. The hind legs are very muscular and are responsible for speed and acceleration. Like all athletes, dogs are susceptible to bone muscle and joint injuries. Lameness and arthritis are common problems in elderly dogs. They also frequently suffer from accidental injuries, causing bone fractures. Generally, it is the hind legs (femur), which get damaged in an accident. Regular exercise and a balanced diet are important for preventing bone and joint disorders.

Why do the front legs of puppies sometimes get bowed?

Bowing of the front legs in puppies is known as rickets and is caused by a deficiency of Vitamin D and an imbalance of calcium/phosphorous

in the diet. Malnutrition and absence of sunlight are contributory factors. The long bones of the front legs (radius and ulna) are primarily affected, and the rib cage may also show nodular swellings. Vitamin D supplements, with a balanced diet containing adequate calcium and phosphorous, help in treating this condition.

What causes lameness of the front legs in dogs?

Fractures, dislocated joints, torn ligaments and tendons, bruised muscles or a bone infection may cause lameness of the front legs. Fractures are generally associated with swelling, and the dog is not able to take any weight on the affected leg. Torn ligaments and tendons are less painful but cause considerable lameness, and bruised muscles are tender to the touch. The head of the dog goes up when the affected front limb touches the ground. Bone infections result from deep penetrating injuries such as dog bites. In road accidents, the shoulder and knee joints are most frequently injured. The lame/injured dog should be taken to the vet for treatment as soon as possible, but the owner should administer emergency first aid immediately.

What are the causes of lameness of the hind legs in dogs?

The most common condition that causes lameness of the hind legs is hip dysplasia, which is a heritable disease. This usually occurs in German Shepherds and other large breeds. Another cause is a ruptured cruciate ligament, which happens suddenly when a dog starts chasing a cat. While there is no satisfactory treatment for dysplasia, one can get a ruptured cruciate ligament surgically treated by a competent vet.

What is the cause of arthritis in dogs and how can one help an arthritic dog?

Arthritis normally affects older dogs and is usually caused by hereditary factors. Overeating and lack of proper exercise predisposes a dog to arthritis, which can also occur due to infections. Larger breeds have a higher incidence of this disorder. Steroids and non-steroidal anti-inflammatory drugs only control chronic arthritis. If arthritis is caused by infection, it requires the administration of antibiotics and painkillers to alleviate the pain and suffering of the affected dog.

What is osteoporosis?

It is a serious disorder that erodes bone strength and density and is caused by a combination of several factors. Osteoporosis is common in dogs that are fed predominantly meat diets. The affected animals do not grow properly and their legs get bowed. They move slowly and feel uncomfortable when touched. An excess of vitamins given to a puppy can also cause osteoporosis. A well-balanced diet containing calcium/phosphorus supplements along with Vitamin D, given to growing puppies, helps in preventing this problem. Milk and cheese are good sources of dietary calcium and should be given to affected puppies and dogs.

Dental Problems

With domestication, dogs do not get the opportunity to use their teeth as much as they had to when they used to hunt and kill in the wild. As a result of this, a large number of pet dogs are affected with gum and tooth diseases by the time they are four to five years old. Gum infection causes bad breath, which sometimes becomes intolerable. Smaller breeds are more prone to gum and tooth diseases than large breeds. Untreated gum disease causes tooth decay. Cleaning the teeth of pet dogs with a toothbrush or a damp cloth every day, along with periodic professional scaling of the teeth by the vet to remove deposited tartar, is essential for preventing tooth and gum diseases.

What are the causes of bad breath in a pet dog?

Tartar deposits on the teeth cause inflammation and infection of the gums. This causes bad breath in dogs. In some breeds, such as Boxers and Bull Terriers, the gums grow and cover the teeth due to an inherited disease of the gums known as proliferative gum disease. Regular scaling of the teeth at four to six-month intervals, to remove the tartar, and having the gum inflammation treated by a vet, helps in preventing bad breath.

Why do some dogs keep drooling or salivate excessively?

Drooling could be caused by a foreign body embedded in the tongue, severe gum and dental infections, a salivary cyst, or injuries to the tongue. A salivary cyst needs to be drained by a vet, who will also remove any foreign bodies, or treat a gum/dental disease.

Do dogs suffering from gum/dental problems need to be on a special diet?

Eating is painful for dogs suffering from these problems, so they should be fed small, soft, chunky pieces of food which do not require chewing.

What is an undershot or overshot jaw condition? Should one keep a puppy affected with either of these problems?

In a normal dog, the upper and lower teeth mesh perfectly when the dog closes his mouth, but if the lower jaw is longer then the upper jaw, it is known as an undershot bite (pig mouth); this is common in Boxers, Bull dogs and Pekingese. In an overshot jaw, it is the upper jaw, which is longer then the lower jaw (parrot mouth); this condition is normally seen in Dobermanns, Dachshunds and Collies. These are congenital defects and affect the bite of the dog. One should check the bite of a puppy and should not select one with either of these two problems. If in doubt, consult your vet.

Do dogs have milk teeth?

Yes, they do. A dog's first teeth are his milk teeth (incisors and canines), which drop out when the puppy is about four and a half to five months old and are replaced by permanent teeth. In some puppies the canine milk teeth do not drop out and the permanent canines come up behind them. It is advisable to get the canine milk teeth extracted by a vet, in order to provide space for the permanent ones.

CONTAGIOUS AND INFECTIOUS DISEASES

Distemper

Canine distemper is a serious and highly infectious viral disease affecting puppies and adult dogs. Puppies of up to six months are more susceptible to this disease, and their mortality rate could be as high as ninety to ninety-five per cent. The distemper virus is discharged in all the secretions/excretions of the affected dog during the acute stage of the illness, and it contaminates the atmosphere, thus making distemper an airborne disease. Therefore, it can be contracted even without actual body contact with the affected animal. The disease starts with a high fever (104°-107°F) and a dirty discharge from the eyes and nostrils. The temperature may come down temporarily, to shoot up again. This is followed by eruptions on the lower part of the abdomen, which develops into pustules. The dog may develop respiratory problems such as bronchitis, pneumonia, vomiting and diarrhoea/dysentery, with a complete loss of appetite. Soon nervous symptoms such as muscular twitching, chorea and paralysis occur, followed by death. Dogs that survive the infection suffer from permanent complications such as constant shaking of the limbs and twitching of the facial muscles (chorea).

Why do dogs that recover from distemper suffer from nervous problems?

The nervous system is more prone to lodge the distemper virus, which then gets localized there, causing damage to the brain cells, as a result of which involuntary twitching of the facial muscles, shaking of the front legs, and even convulsions, may occur.

Is there no effective treatment for distemper?

The distemper virus is not affected by antibiotics so there is no effective treatment for it. However, the secondary bacterial infection, followed by the damage done by the virus, can be checked with the use of antibiotics. Prevention through vaccination is the best way of checking the distemper virus.

Is distemper communicable to human beings?

No, it is not communicable to human beings; the human measles virus vaccine gives cross protection against the distemper virus.

Infectious Canine Hepatitis (ICH)

Infectious canine hepatitis, also known as canine adenovirus, is a serious contagious viral disease which causes hepatitis and sudden death in dogs of all ages. However, puppies are more susceptible to the disease and their mortality rate is very high. The virus is contracted through excretions, such as the urine, faeces and saliva of the affected dog or puppy. The disease starts with persistent vomiting, high fever, and diarrhoea which may contain blood. There is a complete loss of appetite in the affected dog, but he remains very thirsty all the time and wants to drink a lot of water. The tonsils are generally enlarged too. Palpation of the abdomen is painful, especially in the liver region. Haemorrhages may also take place during the prolonged healing period. The affected dog, during recovery, may also show a bluish

discoloration (opacity of the cornea) of the eye. Sometimes the disease may be so serious that the puppy/dog suddenly dies without showing any symptoms.

How does one differentiate between ICH and distemper?

ICH is a contagious disease caused by the adeno group of viruses, and results in severe hepatitis. The liver becomes greatly enlarged, and the symptoms of jaundice are evident. The virus interferes with blood clotting, and haemorrhages are common. Redness of the mucous membranes inside the oral cavity is often evident, and is considered to be a feature which differentiates this disease from distemper. Distemper is an airborne viral disease, which mainly affects the skin and the respiratory, digestive and nervous systems.

Is infectious canine hepatitis communicable to human beings?

No, the ICH virus does not affect human beings and is different from the human hepatitis virus.

Leptospirosis

Leptospirosis is a contagious disease that affects many animals, as well as man, and is caused by a spirochaete (bacteria). Rodents act as the reservoirs of this disease, which is spread by the contamination of water with the urine of rats and infected dogs. Leptospirosis causes jaundice and damage to the kidneys of the affected dogs. It starts with fever, vomiting (sometimes with blood) and diarrhoea. The dog emits a smell similar to urine from his mouth, and the tip of his tongue may show necrosis. He is dull, depressed, unwilling to get up, dehydrated, and may die. The disease, however, responds to antibiotics, if diagnosed on time.

How does one differentiate between leptospirosis, distemper and ICH?

The duration of leptospirosis is much longer than distemper and ICH, which are acute diseases. Leptospirosis responds to antibiotic treatment, whereas distemper and ICH do not.

Is leptospirosis communicable to human beings?

Yes, leptospirosis is communicable to man from infected dogs. The main symptoms are high fever, headache, muscular pain, kidney failure, meningitis and jaundice.

What precautions should one take while handling a case of leptospirosis?

The causative organisms are shed in the urine of affected dogs. Care should be taken to ensure that human beings or dogs do not come in direct contact with the urine of the affected dog, and it does not contaminate food or water. If the sick dog urinates accidentally on the floor, it should be properly cleaned and the area disinfected thoroughly.

Para-influenza

Para-influenza is a viral disease which causes cough and upper respiratory-tract infection in puppies and dogs. The infection is not very serious, and its antigen is incorporated in the combined prophylactic vaccine, given to dogs to protect them from distemper, hepatitis, parvovirus and leptospirosis.

Canine Parvovirus (CPV)

Canine parvovirus is a serious viral disease that causes fatal haemorrhagic gastroenteritis in puppies and adult dogs. Puppies up to the age of twelve to fourteen weeks are most susceptible to parvovirus infection. This disease causes heavy mortality in unvaccinated dogs. It starts with persistent vomiting, loss of appetite, fever and loose motions. This is followed by haemorrhagic gastroenteritis with dysentery. The affected puppies become dehydrated and may die unless treated immediately with intravenous fluid therapy. Very young puppies of five weeks and below develop cardiac problems (myocarditis) and die quickly. Slightly older puppies suffering from the infection respond to treatment, if started in time. Antibiotics are given to control secondary bacterial infection. Vaccination is the best way of preventing this disease, which spreads through food and water contaminated with the faeces of affected dogs. The virus is shed in the faeces, and the faeces should be buried. The diseased puppies/dogs should be kept in isolation.

Do puppies that recover from CPV face any further danger?

Puppies that recover from CPV may suddenly die from cardiac failure since their hearts are permanently damaged. An adult dog that has recovered from CPV may also suffer from malabsorption of nutrients due to permanent damage to the lining of the intestines. They may also suffer from episodes of diarrhoea. Sodium hypochloride is the only chemical that destroys the parvovirus, and should be used in disinfecting the premises of an infected area; the virus can survive up to a year in an infected environment.

Is parvovirus infection communicable to human beings?

No, it is not.

Corona Virus

Corona virus infection also causes severe gastroenteritis, and is slightly less serious than parvovirus. During the course of this disease the dog becomes lethargic and loses appetite, and this is followed by vomiting

and diarrhoea. His faeces emits a foul odour, and the virus is shed in it. There may not be any fever, but secondary bacterial infection may cause complications. Dehydration is common in untreated cases. Mortality is low in adult dogs but higher in puppies. The faeces should be disposed off properly and affected dogs should be isolated.

How does one differentiate between corona virus and parvovirus?

Both diseases cause severe gastroenteritis. The symptoms also overlap, though corona virus is comparatively less severe in nature. The difference can only be detected by a laboratory examination of the infected stool. Corona virus is easily destroyed by heat, whereas parvovirus is heat resistant. The deficiency of white blood cells (leukopaenia) in corona virus is not as much in evidence as in parvovirus. The mortality rate is also lower, though the diarrhoea may persist for a longer time.

Is corona virus communicable to human beings?

No, it is not.

First Aid in Road Accidents and Resuscitation

In an emergency such as a road accident, it may not be possible to get professional veterinary help immediately. As a dog owner, you should be familiar with the basic principles of veterinary first aid required for an injured dog. You should also know how to assess the seriousness of the injury. A first-aid kit should always be kept in the car and in the house to deal with such emergencies. It should contain a pair of scissors, forceps, a thermometer, sterilized gauze, antiseptic cream such as Savlon, antiseptic liquid such as Betadine, antibiotic powder such as Neosporin, Arnica 30 (homeopathic medicine), bandages, adhesive tape and cotton wool.

What should one do if a dog is involved in a car accident?

The first thing to be done is to move the injured dog to the side of the road to prevent him from being hit by moving traffic. However, you have to be very careful in handling a seriously injured dog, as he may become aggressive and bite. Comfort the dog from a distance and control the traffic. Move the dog only after winning his confidence. Try and muzzle him with a scarf/rope/neck tie to prevent him from biting you. After moving him to one side, assess the seriousness of his condition. If the dog is unconscious, straighten his neck and open his mouth. Gently pull his tongue out so that it does not block his throat, and he can breathe freely. If the bleeding is profuse, control it by applying digital pressure and a bandage over the wound, after cleaning it with Betadine liquid, if available. Watch the dog's chest movements to see if he is breathing. Also check his pulse on the inside of the hind leg. (The heartbeat can also be felt by pressing the hand firmly on the chest, behind the elbow.) If the dog is in shock, his breathing and heart rate will increase (the normal respiration rate is twenty to thirty breaths per minute; and the heart rate fifty to one hundred and fifty beats per minute), depending on the size of the dog. A dog suffering from shock should be kept warm, and should be lifted gently and taken to the nearest veterinary clinic.

How does one know whether the dog is dead or unconscious? Is there anything one can do to revive him?

Check the dog's chest to find out whether he is breathing, and feel his pulse and heartbeat. Shine a torch into his eye, and if the pupil contracts, the dog is alive. You can also pinch the toe of one of the hind legs, and if there is no response, it means that the dog is either deeply unconscious or dead. He will deflect his foot if he is even slightly conscious.

What is shock and how does one recognize it?

Shock occurs when body circulation fails. The dog becomes weak, is cold to the touch, and his pulse and breathing are very fast. A dog in a state of shock must be kept warm and rushed to the nearest veterinary clinic for professional help. Internal haemorrhage is invariably the cause of sudden shock.

What precautions should one take while taking a dog injured in a car accident to a veterinary clinic?

After administering basic first aid, the dog should be lifted using a blanket as a stretcher, and this should then be wrapped around him. He should be put down on the car seat, with head extended and tongue pulled out, and then administered a dose of Arnica 30. If the dog is partially conscious, the owner should comfort him by sitting near him. One should not unnecessarily touch an injured dog, and a detailed examination should be left to the vet.

What precautions should one take to prevent road accidents while walking with one's pet?

Make sure that your dog is kept on a leash and is trained to walk at heel on your left. Always keep him under control on a busy road, and be especially careful while crossing it.

Should one take a dog that has been involved in an accident for a veterinary check-up if it does not have any visible external signs of injury?

One should always take a dog that has been involved in an accident for a thorough veterinary check-up, as sometimes there may be internal bleeding, or the dog may have post-accidental concussion. He should be kept under observation for at least twenty-four hours.

How does one know whether a dog that has been involved in an accident has suffered serious internal bleeding?

If the injured dog is unconscious but breathing, expose the gums and press them with a finger to see if the blood returns soon after you remove your finger. If it does not, it could be due to severe internal bleeding.

Does cardiac massage and artificial respiration help if the heart and respiration of the injured dog has stopped?

It does sometimes. Massage the area on the left side of the chest, behind the elbow of the left leg. Place your open palm over the dog's heart area, and placing the other hand on top, press firmly with both hands down and forwards towards the head. This squeezes blood out of the heart to the brain. Repeat at one-second intervals for at least ten minutes. Administer artificial respiration, if you can, by holding the nose of the dog with both your hands, and blowing into the nostrils for about three seconds to inflate the lungs. If correctly done, the chest will expand; pause for two seconds and repeat. This is called mouth-to-nose respiration to revive breathing. Continue alternating cardiac massage with artificial respiration till the heart starts beating.

How does one administer first aid to a drowning dog?

Sometimes dogs go into deep water from where they are unable to get out. After getting tired they swallow a lot of water and lose consciousness. You should first drain out the water by holding the dog upside down by his hind legs. Shake him, and if he is not breathing, lay him on his side and give artificial respiration followed by cardiac massage. One should fence off swimming pools to prevent such accidents.

Checklist for Road Accidents

- Gently move the injured dog to the side of the road.

- Check if he is alive or dead.
- Clear the air passage by opening the mouth, removing the saliva, and ensuring that the tongue is outside the mouth.
- Give cardiac massage if the heart has stopped beating, and follow it by administering artificial respiration.
- Control severe external bleeding by bandaging bleeding wounds, applying a little pressure.
- Do not handle fractured limbs.
- Lift the injured dog, using a blanket as a stretcher.
- Keep the dog warm, wrapped in a blanket, while taking him to the vet.
- Give him a dose of Arnica 30.
- Always keep a first-aid kit handy in your car and house.
- Always take your dog out on a leash and train him to walk at heel on your left.
- Fence off swimming pools to prevent puppies/dogs from accidentally drowning.

Euthanasia (Mercy Killing)

Dogs sometimes suffer from incurable disorders or diseases. Instead of prolonging their agony and letting them suffer, it is prudent to accept your vet's advice regarding euthanasia (putting an incurably sick or very old dog to sleep painlessly). Euthanasia is a medical privilege, a gift that can be lovingly bestowed on a dying or incurably sick dog, treating him with the respect and love he deserves. There is no doubt that for the owner it is painful to watch a loved dog die, but it is advisable that he or she is present at this time, to be with him at the end and bid him a loving good-bye. In this way the dog can die peacefully without any pain. It has been observed that those owners who are not with their dogs at this time suffer from greater distress at the loss of their pets. In any case, a caring owner would not wish to abandon his dog at such a time. In such cases, the vet informs the owner about the preparations required and administering a short-acting barbiturate intravenously, carries out euthanasia. It is a totally painless procedure, and the dog dies immediately. Some people may think it is cruel, but in fact it is the most humane and painless method of ending the suffering of a terminally sick dog.

What preparations are generally required for euthanasia?

The following is the normal procedure for euthanasia:

- A suitable time convenient for both the owner and the vet, should be fixed.
- A suitable box/blanket is required to transport the body of the dog afterwards.
- The owner should bring one or two close friends or relatives to provide moral support.
- Arrangements for disposing off the body by burial/cremation should be made.
- The vet's bill should be settled in advance.

How does one dispose of the body of a pet dog?

Burial is the most common way of disposing of the body of a pet dog. Sufficient lime powder and salt should be poured over the dog's body before covering it with soil. The pit in which the dog is buried should be at least four feet deep, so that animals cannot dig it out. Some people prefer to cremate their pets.

The municipal authority in New Delhi, the NDMC, has an electric crematorium for pets at its veterinary hospital at Motibagh.

zoonosis: diseases transmitted from dog to man

Zoonosis is another term for diseases that are transmitted to man from animals. Pet dogs have the closest contact with humans, and due to this proximity, can transmit several diseases to humans if proper precautions are not taken. Zoonotic diseases in India affect a large number of pet owners (especially children), mainly because of a lack of proper hygiene and unsanitary conditions. The hot and humid climatic conditions further aggravate the problem. A large stray-dog population also poses a threat to human beings and the environment in India. However, except for rabies, the majority of dog-transmitted diseases are not very serious; most are preventable and can be easily cured if diagnosed properly. Though there are a number of infections which can be contracted from dogs, only those responsible for causing serious health hazards are being dealt with in this book.

Serious diseases/infections, which can be passed on by dogs to human beings in addition to rabies are brucellosis, leptospirosis, ringworm, asthma, hookworms, roundworms, hydated cysts and plague. Rabies is the worst of all zoonotic diseases, and has already been discussed in detail.

Rabies and Dog Bites

Rabies is perhaps the most dreaded communicable disease contracted by human beings from animals, and the death rate is a hundred per cent. Dogs are the principal carriers of this disease in India. It has been estimated that around 30,000 people die of rabies every year, and more than a million have to be administered post-bite rabies vaccination. All warm-blooded animals are susceptible to the disease, which is transmitted mainly through the bite or lick of a rabid dog. It can also be transmitted to human beings through the bite of a rabid cat. The virus is present in the saliva of the rabid dog/cat. The rabies virus can enter the body not only through a bite or wound but also through the healthy and intact mucous membranes of the mouth, eyes, nose and rectum. After entering the body, the virus travels through the nerves to the brain, where it causes encephalitis, leading to death. The saliva of a rabid dog becomes infected a few days before the appearance of clinical symptoms, and the incubation period of the virus varies from about seven days to several months, depending on the severity and location of the bite. The psychological trauma is severe, and people fear that every dog bite will cause rabies. Several countries, such as the UK and Australia, have been able to eradicate rabies by implementing stringent control and quarantine measures.

In human beings, the disease is referred to as hydrophobia (fear of water). This is due to the fact that when a hydrophobia patient tries to drink water, sudden spasms of the throat muscles make the person feel that he/she is choking. Initially, there is depression, headache, anxiety, and pain at the site of the dog bite. This slowly leads to exhaustion, paralysis and death.

In dogs, the disease manifests itself either in 'furious' or 'dumb' form. In the 'furious' form, there is a pronounced period of excitement, during which the rabid animal runs about like a mad creature and bites anyone who comes in his way. Initially, the symptoms are excessive salivation, a vacant look in the eyes, hiding in dark corners of the house, and snapping at imaginary objects such as flies. The dog

may also start biting his own chain. Stray dogs travel long distances, running aimlessly with long strings of saliva dropping from half-open mouths. Eventually paralysis of the hindquarters, followed by convulsions and death, occurs within four to five days. Pet dogs generally suffer from the 'dumb' form of rabies, but a few may have the 'furious' form. These dogs may recognize their master for some time, but later start biting their chains or leashes and attacking everyone. In the 'dumb' form of the disease, the dog becomes very quiet and has a dull, lack-lustre appearance. He may show no interest in food and his surroundings. This is followed by difficulty in swallowing. The main symptoms are profuse salivation, with the tongue hanging out, and paralysis of the lower jaw. Finally, the hindquarters are paralyzed and death follows.

There is no treatment for rabies, either for human beings or animals, therefore preventive vaccination of dogs is most important, as is the post-bite treatment, both for man and dog. Since the disease is spread through the bite of rabid dogs/cats, controlling the stray dog/cat population and vaccinating them is of great importance to the eradication of the disease.

How is rabies transmitted to human beings and animals?

Rabies can be transmitted to human beings in any of the following ways:

- Being bitten by a rabid dog, cat or jackal.
- Contamination of a wound, cut or bruise by the saliva of an infected animal.
- Contamination of the intact mucous membranes of the mouth, eye, nose and rectum by the saliva of the infected animal.
- Contamination of broken skin, a wound or mucous membrane, by the body fluids (such as milk and urine) of the rabid animal.

What precautions should one take after being bitten by an unknown dog?

Being bitten by any dog, especially an unknown stray dog, can have serious consequences, and the following action should be taken at once:

- Immediately wash the bite wound with plenty of soap and water. Then clean it with alcohol/whiskey and apply liquid Betadine; do not bandage the wound or get it stitched.
- Contact your family physician and ask him to administer at least five post-exposure anti-rabies injections (on days 0, 3, 7, 14 and 30 after being bitten), and also tetanus injections. It is absolutely necessary to start the treatment as soon as possible. Day 0 is the day the first injection should be administered; this is the day the person is bitten by the dog.
- If possible, keep the dog under observation in a separate kennel/ room for at least ten days; a rabid dog will die within this period. Offer him food and water from a distance. If the dog is rabid, he will show clinical symptoms of the disease, such as paralysis, and will die.

What precautions should one take after being accidentally bitten by one's pet dog that has been vaccinated with anti-rabies vaccine?

Being bitten by one's own dog that has been vaccinated with anti-rabies vaccine is normally not a cause of concern, especially if the dog has not been exposed to stray dogs. However, you should immediately wash the bite with soap and water, apply spirit/alcohol, and take the dog to the vet for a check-up and advice. The vet will want to know the circumstances under which the dog bit you. After examining him, he will advise you regarding anti-tetanus inoculation,

as well as provide three post-exposure anti-rabies injections if required, while keeping the dog under observation.

If one's vaccinated pet dog is bitten by another vaccinated pet dog, should post-exposure anti-rabies vaccination be administered to one's dog?

Although being bitten by a vaccinated pet dog is not considered dangerous, to be on the safe side, one should start post-exposure anti-rabies treatment immediately and keep the dog under observation. Your vet will be the best person to advise you.

If a stray dog bites a vaccinated dog, does he require post-exposure vaccination?

Yes, he does. You must immediately consult your vet and have a full course of five post-exposure anti-rabies injections administered to your dog on days 0, 3, 7, 14 and 30 (post bite). At the same time try and keep the stray dog under observation for ten days.

Why is post-exposure vaccination essential for a vaccinated dog whose vaccination schedule is up to date?

While anti-rabies vaccination provides immunity against rabies, it may not ensure a hundred per cent protection against the bite of a rabid dog. Therefore, you will need to give your pet dog a series of five anti-rabies booster shots to boost his immunity and ensure hundred per cent protection against rabies. Considering the seriousness of the disease, do not ever take chances with it.

How does one protect one's puppy/dog against rabies?

The first inoculation against rabies is given to a puppy when he is three months old. A booster shot is given after six months, that is, at nine months of age. After this, annual booster shots are administered. Live-virus anti-rabies vaccines are not recommended, and one should use killed-virus anti-rabies vaccines only. Raksha-rab is a reliable anti-rabies vaccine manufactured by Indian Immunologicals. Several vets use imported anti-rabies vaccines manufactured by reputed manufacturers, which are also very reliable. The first inoculation against rabies for puppies born to an unvaccinated mother should be given at four to five weeks of age, followed by a booster at twelve weeks, and a third booster at nine months.

What are the anti-rabies vaccines available for humans?

The old nervous-tissue origin anti-rabies vaccine, when fourteen painful injections had to be given in the abdomen, is now obsolete. Much better and safer anti-rabies vaccines are now available for intra-muscular use in India. They are:

- Human diploid cell-culture anti-rabies vaccine (MIRV-HDC Serum International), both for pre-and post-exposure immunization
- Verorab (Cadila Pharma), for pre-and post-exposure immunization
- Verovax-R (Aventis Pasteur) vaccine for pre-and post-exposure immunization
- Rabipur (Behring) for pre-and post-exposure immunization

What is pre-exposure immunization for rabies?

Human beings, especially vets, who are exposed to a high risk of contracting rabies, are advised pre-exposure or primary immunization by the administration of three anti-rabies injections on days 0, 7 and 28. A booster shot is given every two years.

What is the procedure for post-bite immunization of human beings?

A person bitten by a stray dog that cannot be observed or located should take six anti-rabies injections on days 0, 3, 7, 14, 30 and 90. However, if the dog is a pet and has been vaccinated, and can be kept under observation, only three post-exposure anti-rabies injections on

days 0, 3 and 7 after the bite will be required. Do not take any more injections if the dog remains healthy 10 days after day 0.

When should human beings start taking anti-rabies injections?

Anti-rabies injections should be started immediately after a person is bitten or even licked under the following conditions:

- The dog shows clinical signs of rabies.
- It has been tested positive for rabies by a laboratory examination.
- The dog is suspected of having rabies, even though the laboratory result is negative.
- Following a bite by a stray/pet dog.
- After handling a rabid animal when even a minor abrasion on the skin could have been contaminated by its saliva.

Should one start anti-rabies treatment even after being bitten by an apparently healthy dog that has been vaccinated?

Yes, appropriate treatment should be started at once, that is, at least three injections on days 0, 3 and 7 after being bitten. It should be discontinued if the animal is alive and healthy on the tenth day. If, however, the animal develops symptoms even remotely resembling rabies during the ten-day observation period, the full course of six injections should be administered. The vet and the family physician should, however, be consulted before taking a final decision.

What are the indications for starting anti-rabies serum treatment?

Anti-rabies hyper immune serum is very efficacious and should be given in all cases of severe rabid-dog bites, especially on or near the head. It should be administered immediately after exposure. Whether the patient has been given the serum or not, it is essential that anti-rabies treatment is also started with the least possible delay.

Can one get rabies by drinking the milk of an animal (cow/buffalo) suffering from rabies?

Drinking un-boiled milk from an animal suffering from rabies can expose you to infection. Boiling kills the virus, therefore boiled milk is safe.

Can one get rabies by eating the meat of a rabid animal, or one that has died of rabies?

Only eating uncooked/semi-cooked meat can infect you. Proper cooking destroys the virus, and therefore there is no danger of contracting the disease by eating properly cooked meat.

Can one get rabies if one has been bitten through clothing?

You can get infected even if you are bitten through clothing. However, it has been found that the mortality rate of rabies patients is three times higher for those bitten on bare skin as compared to those bitten through clothing.

Are the chances of getting rabies the same from different species of animals?

No, they are not the same. Wolf bites are the most dangerous, followed by jackal, dog and cat bites. Horses and cattle rarely transmit the disease. Human saliva can be infectious, though rarely. However, considering the seriousness of the disease, always take the full course of post-exposure injections, irrespective of the animal by which you have been bitten.

Can a monkey bite transmit rabies?

Being bitten by a healthy monkey will not cause rabies. However, if a rabid dog has bitten the monkey he can contract and transmit rabies to human beings and other animals by biting them. Rabies has been recorded in monkeys.

Apart from the post-exposure anti-rabies vaccination, what other precautions should one take after being bitten by a rabid animal?

Anti-tetanus injections must be administered, and the patient should avoid strenuous manual labour. Nourishing food must be eaten during this period, and alcohol should be strictly avoided.

Are there any adverse effects of the anti-rabies vaccination?

Present-day vaccines are absolutely safe and there are no adverse effects whatsoever.

How can one diagnose rabies in a dog?

The most valuable diagnostic feature of the disease in a dog is the short duration of the illness, which is always followed by death. The symptoms of rabies are very clear and an experienced vet can easily diagnose the disease with reasonable accuracy. However, the disease can only be confirmed after a microscopic examination of the brain and biological laboratory tests. An animal suspected of suffering from rabies should not be killed, but should be placed under observation in an isolated room. If he has rabies, he will die within four to five days of showing the classic symptoms of the disease.

If a pet dog (which has not been vaccinated with anti-rabies vaccine) is exposed to rabies by being bitten by a rabid dog, can he be fully protected with post-exposure anti-rabies treatment?

Owing to their susceptibility to rabies, and its relatively short incubation period in dogs, complete reliance cannot be placed on post-exposure vaccination of unvaccinated dogs. Even if such dogs are given six post-exposure anti-rabies injections, they are liable to develop rabies any time up to a year from when they were bitten, though the first three months are the most critical. Moreover, it is risky to keep such dogs, even after treatment, if one has children in the house. Therefore, it is advisable that unvaccinated dogs, that are severely bitten (or bitten near the head by a rabid dog), should be put to sleep. However, if the owner decides not to destroy the dog, strict isolation of the animal in a kennel/separate room for a period of six months is essential.

Since the incidence of this deadly disease is highest in India, what action should be taken to control it?

The following measures should be taken to control the high incidence of rabies in India:

- Rabies should be controlled in dogs, in order to check the disease in human beings.
- The population of stray dogs should be controlled by spaying/neutering.
- There should be compulsory vaccination and registration of all pet dogs.
- Rabies should be declared as a notifiable disease in humans and animals.
- Public education advocating the adoption of community dogs as pets, and vaccinating them, will help in controlling the disease.
- Diagnostic facilities for rabies should be made more efficient.
- The stray dog population should be vaccinated with the aid of municipal bodies.
- Municipal bodies should have isolation/kennelling facilities for dogs.
- There should be a national rabies control committee to coordinate the rabies control programme.
- Strict quarantine should be imposed on all imports.
- A geographical survey should be carried out regarding the

prevalence of rabies in India, in order to implement the control programme effectively.

- There should be a strict check on the movement of dogs from neighbouring countries such as Pakistan, Bangladesh, Nepal and Bhutan, to India.

Brucellosis

Brucellosis is primarily a disease of cattle, causing abortions. Human beings can contract if by drinking infected milk and through household pets. The causative organism, B.canis, which affects dogs, is also pathogenic to human beings. Humans are infected by contact with the secretions/uterine discharge of infected dogs suffering from the disease.

What are the symptoms of brucellosis in humans?

Fever, headache and joint pain are the first symptoms, followed by complications such as pneumonia and meningitis if the disease is not treated with suitable antibiotics in the early stages.

What are the symptoms of brucellosis in dogs?

The commonest sign of brucellosis is sudden abortion in female dogs and infertility in males. Most often, abortion occurs during the last stages of pregnancy in an otherwise healthy female dog. Puppies born to them are usually weak and do not survive to weaning age. In male dogs, infertility and inflammation of the testes is common three to five weeks after they are infected. The affected animals show no sign of discomfort unless the scrotal contents are palpated.

How does a dog suffering from brucellosis infect human beings?

Direct contact with aborted foetal material, uterine discharge, and the urine of an infected dog infects human beings. Observing proper hygiene and sanitary measures can prevent transmission of brucellosis from dogs to human beings.

Leptospirosis

This disease can be transmitted from animals to human beings by physical contact with their droppings/urine, and also by consuming food and water contaminated with infected urine. In humans it can cause fever, jaundice and even renal failure. The disease is prevalent in India, especially in Gujarat and Maharashtra. Rats and bandicoots are the main carriers of the disease. In dogs it is caused by *Leptospira canicola* and *Leptospira icterohaemorrhagiae*, which are spirochaetes. Fortunately, a preventive vaccine is available for dogs; therefore make sure that your pet gets yearly booster shots, apart from the primary vaccination schedule of three injections. Leptospirosis is considered to be one of the most widespread zoonotic diseases in the world, particularly in underdeveloped and developing countries.

What is the commonest source of human infection?

Infected animals shed the organisms of the disease in their urine, therefore contamination or contact with the infected urine results in human infection. The organism can enter through abrasions in the skin and mucous membranes. Person-to-person spread of infection rarely occurs. (See also pages 160-161.)

Ringworm

Ringworm is a common fungal infection that dogs get. It can be transmitted back and forth between human beings and their dogs by direct contact with the infected animal/person or infected clothing. Dog's hair and skin should be kept in good condition by regular brushing and periodic grooming, and matted hair should be trimmed.

Immediate action should be taken to get ringworms treated in pet dogs.

Asthma

Many dog owners are sensitive to dandruff in dogs. Children are especially susceptible, and this can trigger an asthmatic attack. It is not advisable for asthmatic people, sensitive to dandruff in dogs, to keep them as pets. All dog owners should ensure that their animals are well groomed and periodically bathed to prevent an accumulation of dandruff/dust in their coats.

Hookworm (Cutaneous Larval Migrans)

Hookworms are common intestinal parasites in dogs. Their eggs are passed out in the dog's faeces, and hatch in the soil into tiny larvae, which are capable of piercing human skin. Having entered the skin, they cause an intensely itchy rash. Periodic deworming of puppies and adult dogs against hookworms is needed to prevent human infection. Walking barefoot on the grass and infected ground in public parks, which is generally contaminated with the faeces of stray/pet dogs, is the commonest way of contracting hookworm infection. The faeces of pet dogs should be immediately removed and properly disposed off to prevent contamination of lawns. Children who play on contaminated lawns or suffer from pica (eating soil) are most vulnerable to hookworm infection. (See also page 141.)

Roundworm (Visceral Larval Migrans)

Of all the roundworms that infect dogs, one species, ascaris (*Toxocara canis*), is of zoonotic relevance. This is the most common canine worm that infects human beings. Human infection can take place through

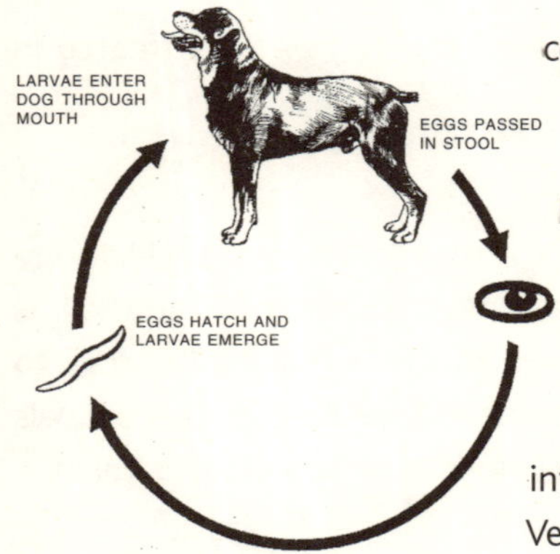

LIFE CYCLE OF ROUNDWORMS

contact with soil containing even traces of dog faeces, and then eating food with contaminated hands. Children who play in public parks contaminated with the faeces of stray/pet dogs, and then eat their food without washing their hands, pick up infection by swallowing the eggs. Very small children sometimes eat contaminated soil while playing, and get infected. Playing with infested puppies/adult dogs, and then eating without properly washing your hands is another way of contracting roundworm infection from dogs.

How do the ingested eggs/larvae of roundworms harm human beings?

After human beings ingest the eggs, the eggs hatch and liberate the second stage larvae in the intestines. Since humans are non-specific hosts of dog roundworms, these second-stage larvae do not undergo further development, and migrate from the intestines to the liver, lungs, brain and eyes. In human beings, this can cause enlargement of the liver. Children from one to four years of age are especially susceptible. The migrating larvae can reach the eyes, causing blindness. They can also cause pneumonia.

How can one prevent children from getting infected by canine roundworm eggs?

Small children (one to four years of age) should not be allowed to play on ground/grass that has been contaminated by the faeces of stray pet

CHILDREN PICK UP ROUNDWORMS FROM CONTAMINATED GROUND

dogs. They must also be supervised and made to wash their hands thoroughly after playing with or handling puppies/adult dogs. The faeces of puppies and adult dogs should be properly disposed off immediately by burying them, and children should be forbidden to play with stray puppies, as they are usually heavily infested with roundworms.

Puppies and even some adult dogs love to lick children on their mouth. Is this harmful?

Puppies and adult dogs should not be allowed to lick children or adults on the mouth. Dogs have a dirty habit of licking their anus, and during the process pick up roundworm eggs on their tongue and muzzle. This can be easily passed on to children when they lick them. A puppy suffering from diarrhoea can contaminate the whole house.

How can one control roundworm *(Toxocara canis)* infection in puppies/adult dogs?

Most puppies contract roundworm infection even before they are born. They also get infected through their mother's milk. By the time the puppies are four weeks old, they start shedding roundworm eggs, which are infectious for human beings, in their stool. Therefore, deworming them against roundworms when they are three to four weeks old is essential. This should be repeated two weeks later. The mother dog should also be dewormed with her puppies, as cleaning her puppies will infect her. Pregnant female dogs should also be dewormed (for roundworms and hookworms) when they are four weeks pregnant, to ensure that the puppies are not born with toxocara (roundworm) infection. Proper disposal of dog faeces is an effective measure in preventing roundworm infection in humans and dogs.

Checklist for Preventing Toxocara Infection in Children

- Ensure that children always wash their hands before they eat.
- Discourage children from putting dirty fingers into their mouths.
- Do not allow children to play on the ground in public places, because they are usually contaminated with the faeces of dogs with roundworm infestation.
- Be sure that floors on which children play are clean.
- Do not leave small children on the floor at the entrance of public buildings frequented by dogs.
- Do not keep children unsupervised with a puppy or dog, unless it is over six months old.
- Always dispose off the dog faeces immediately if he defecates inside the house.
- If possible, fence the children's playground, so as to keep away stray dogs that can contaminate the soil.

Hydatid Cysts (Echinococcosis)

The dog tapeworm, *echinococcus granulosus*, has special relevance from the zoonotic point of view. Humans get infected by ingesting the eggs of the adult tapeworm from contaminated hands or by being licked by infected dogs. Stroking a dog's contaminated fur can also infect humans, especially children. Dog owners are also vulnerable to the infection when grooming the dogs, if they do not wash their hands properly afterwards. Food and water, or public parks contaminated with

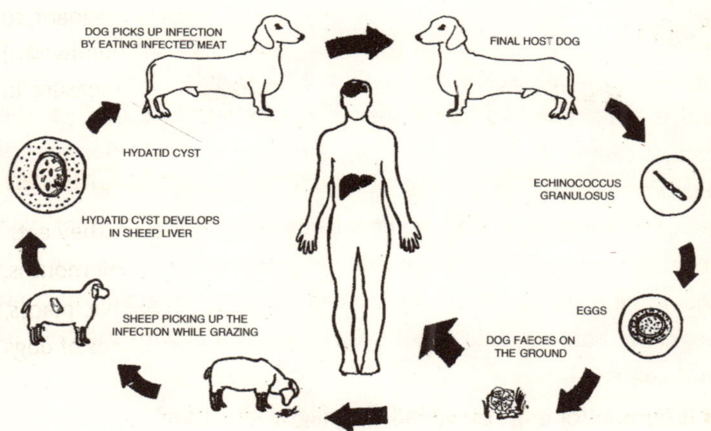

LIFE CYCLE OF ECHINOCOCCUS

infected dog faeces, can also be a source of infection. After human beings ingest canine tapeworm eggs, the larvae (from the eggs) migrate from the intestines to various organs of the body and form cysts called hydatid cysts.

How do hydatid cysts affect human beings?

The mechanical pressure exerted by the cysts on the surrounding tissue causes clinical signs in humans. The symptoms vary with the size and location of the cysts. These cysts may result in jaundice, severe headache, epileptic fits, and many other health problems, depending on the organ affected.

How does one prevent echinococcosis infection in human beings?

Observing proper hygiene and sanitary measures can do this, and keeping one's pet free from tapeworm infection. Children should not be allowed to play on ground that may be contaminated with dog faeces.

Plague

Plague is a fatal disease caused by a bacillus called *yersinia pestis*, and is transmitted to human beings by the bite of a rat flea. The natural carriers of this flea are domestic and wild rats. Sometimes fleas from domestic rats start living on pet dogs, and also attack human beings. Keeping dogs free from fleas by using flea collars and anti-flea shampoos/soaps are therefore absolutely necessary measures, which should be used to prevent the spread of plague infection through dogs. The house should also be kept free of rats with the help of pest control.

Is it normal for dogs to spread the plague infection?

Dogs are not natural carriers of the plague, but they sometimes accidentally harbour rat fleas, which can be the source of this infection.

Checklist for Communicable Diseases

Following the simple precautions given below can considerably reduce the risk of contracting communicable diseases from dogs. You should also discuss with your vet the possibility of getting an infection/disease from your pet dog. Dog owners should always strictly adhere to routine measures, which ensure hygiene and sanitation and prevent the spread of communicable diseases by pet dogs.

- Always make sure that your dog is vaccinated in time and regularly, especially for rabies.
- Regular periodic deworming of puppies/adult dogs is absolutely necessary for preventing the spread of worm infections.
- Always wash your (and your children's) hands before eating.
- Never allow your children to play with stray puppies or dogs.
- Do not allow children to play on ground contaminated with the faeces of stray/pet dogs.

- Do not walk barefoot in public parks contaminated with the faeces of stray/pet dogs.
- Never allow your children to kiss puppies or dogs on their mouths or snouts.
- Bury dog faeces immediately after the dog defecates.
- Do not allow your dog to dirty playgrounds, parks and public places. Owners should remove the dog faeces from these places, should their pets accidentally defecate there.
- Do not allow a pet dog suffering from diarrhoea to come in contact with children.
- After a bout of diarrhoea, bathe your dog properly to decontaminate his hair coat.
- Rubber gloves should be worn while administering oral medication to pet dogs, to avoid being bitten accidentally.
- Dogs should not be allowed to lick wounds on the human body.
- Keep your dog clean, properly groomed, periodically bathed, and free from ticks/fleas.
- Groom your dog outside the house, and sweep the area clean, so as to remove the dandruff and fallen hair immediately.
- Do not allow your dog to sleep on your bed.
- Keep the dog's living area clean and free from dirt, uneaten food, and excrement.
- Provide a proper bed in a basket or box for your dog outside your bedroom.
- Communicable diseases are more frequently contracted from puppies than adult dogs.
- Immuno-suppressed people should be extremely careful about keeping a dog as a pet.

- Get your dog regularly checked up by your vet, to ensure that he remains in good health.
- Consult your vet immediately if your dog is even slightly ill.
- A newly-acquired dog or puppy should be thoroughly examined by a vet before inducting him into the family.

alternative systems of health care

Alternative systems of health care, such as homeopathy, herbal treatment, acupuncture/acupressure and massage, are becoming increasingly popular these days. Many vets use these alternative systems along with allopathic medicines when treating pets.

Homeopathic Remedies

Homeopathic remedies have certain advantages over conventional allopathic medicines, as they are cheaper and easier to administer. Homeopathy is as effective for dogs as it is for human beings. However, to get the full benefit of this system, a great deal of study, observation, and consultation with qualified practising homeopaths/physicians is required. Homeopathic remedies produce good results when judiciously used in some common ailments in dogs. A good homeopath is skilled in prescribing the right remedy, based on the symptoms of the illness. When the right medicine is administered, results can be miraculous. Homeopathic remedies come in the X (10th) dilution and C (100th) dilution for home use; doctors sometimes use higher potencies. X dilutions are considered to be slower-acting and less long-lasting than C dilutions. For example, a 6X is less potent than a 12X, and a 6C less than a 12C. Homeopathic medicine doses are the same for everyone, but the potency varies. It is advisable to use lower-potency medicines (6X and 12X), and administer the doses more often. In an acute case, the dose can be repeated every 15 minutes (up to four doses), then every two hours up to another four

doses. The doses should be administered thrice or four times a day, for a few days, for less serious ailments. For chronic diseases, the medicine should be given thrice a day for four to seven days; then wait and repeat the course, if necessary. This is meant to be a general guide for dog owners so that they can administer first-aid treatment with homeopathic medicines (in an emergency only), while waiting for the vet to treat their dogs. These medicines are particularly successful in treating asthma, allergy and skin disorders. Therefore, the following conditions/ailments (which call for emergency first aid) have been selected, so that owners can administer homeopathic treatment to their dogs at home.

Accidents

In an accident, there is always an element of shock accompanied by bleeding from cuts and wounds, which is associated with pain. Arnica-30 (3X) successfully treats shock, haemorrhage and pain from bruising. Give the dog five to six globules directly on the tongue, or dissolve them in a tablespoon of slightly warm water and administer this to him every two hours. Aconite-30 can also be given every 15 minutes as a first-aid measure.

Allergy

Allergy can be caused by many factors, such as pesticides/food/pollen/insect bites, and so forth. The dog's eyes become red and urticarial eruptions may develop all over his body. Give him Euphrasia-30, or Urtica-30 (five to six globules with warm water) for these problems. Rhustox is efficacious for itching and burning rashes, and Aconite for severe allergic conditions. Carboveg is recommended when the dog's breathing is impaired.

Loss of Appetite

If your dog refuses to eat, but seems to be fit, i.e., he is alert and active, you should not worry for a day or two. A healthy dog is normally a hungry dog, and he should begin eating normally soon. However, for minor digestive upsets, when he walks away from his food, he can be given Arsenic-30 at hourly intervals. Nux-vomica-30 can also be given.

Vomiting

A dog vomiting occasionally is not a cause for concern, but if he vomits repeatedly he needs to be treated professionally by a vet. Merc-cor-30, Arnica-30 and Nux-vomica-30 may be tried in cases of persistent vomiting.

Diarrhoea

Dogs have a habit of eating anything and everything; therefore, they sometimes suffer from diarrhoea, sometimes accompanied by vomiting. Arsenicum-30 and Merc-cor-30 can be given to them for these disorders.

Constipation

Older dogs tend to suffer from constipation. It is also a condition common in dogs after they have eaten bones. Nux-vomica-30 and Carboveg-30 are effective for this problem.

Fever and Cough

A dog with fever is normally dull, with an increased rate of respiration, accompanied by greater thirst and loss of appetite. This could also be the first sign of an infectious/contagious disease. Therefore, a dog that has fever needs urgent veterinary attention. However, as a first aid, you can administer Aconite-30 and Gelsemium-30 at half-hourly intervals. If fever is accompanied by coughing, give the dog Bryonia-30 or Rhus-tox-30.

Ear Problems

Pain in the ear could be an emergency if the slightest touch to the ear causes the dog pain and discomfort. He may cry out suddenly, and may constantly scratch the affected ear. Repeat Chamomilla-30 every hour.

Haematoma of the Ear

A dog shaking his head vigorously sometimes results in damage/ rupture of the blood vessels in the earflap, which gets swollen due to accumulation of blood. Arnica-30 can be given thrice a day. However, this is a serious condition and may require surgery.

Eye Problems

Conjunctivitis is a common eye problem in dogs. Euphrasia-30 or Arsenic-30 can be given for this disorder.

Fits or Epilepsy

Dogs occasionally suffer from fits/epilepsy. It is a serious problem, which needs a thorough investigation/examination by a vet. However, you may use Cocculus-30 or Scutellaria-30 after consulting your vet.

Flatulence

Dogs sometimes suffer from excessive accumulation of gas in the stomach, which results in rumbling sounds in the abdomen. Use Carboveg-30 and Nux-vomica-30 for this problem.

Hiccups

Hiccups are common in puppies. Nux-vomica-30 may be used to treat this disorder.

Mange/Dermatitis

The affected dog scratches incessantly due to the intense irritation caused by the mange mites. This is a serious condition and needs proper investigation and treatment by a vet. However, Sulphur-30 and Arsenic-30 may help.

Sneezing

Sneezing can be a symptom of an allergy. Arsenic-30 and Gelsemium-30 may be tried for this problem.

Pain

Dogs suffering from acute pain are restless; they pant and sometimes groan with pain. Hypericum-30 and Chamomilla-30 can help if the pain is caused by a toothache/back injury/cold.

Whelping

Homeopathic medicines can be administered to your dog while she is giving birth; it will help her deliver her puppies without any difficulty. Pulsatilla-30 and Arnica-30 are efficacious for this.

Pining (crying when left alone)

Some dogs cannot bear to be separated from their owners and bark/cry when left alone. Pulsatilla-30 may be given for this. However, for a pet that is grieving or pining, Ignatia-30 is a better remedy.

Shock/Collapse

If your dog suddenly collapses, and there is a bluish discoloration of the tongue and mucous membranes, Carboveg-30 may be given as emergency first aid until a vet is available.

Stings

Bees, wasps and other insects may sting puppies or dogs. Apis-mel-30 or Cantheris-30 can be used for this.

Wounds

Calendula lotion has good healing properties, and should be applied twice or thrice a day on wounds/cuts. Arnica-30 and Hypericum-30 can be given orally.

Herbal Drugs

Plants, as a source of medicines, have been used from time immemorial. It is one of the oldest systems of healing discovered and developed by primitive man to keep him healthy and treat ailments. However, with the passage of time, the secrets of many herbal drugs were forgotten, and allopathic medicines came to dominate the scene. During the last few decades, herbal remedies have regained their lost value and importance in treating humans as well as animals.

Domestic and wild animals eat plants naturally when they need medication or internal cleaning. Every dog owner has observed his dog eating grass or selected weeds to promote and induce vomiting. This process helps the dog treat his digestive disorders. Wild animals know what plants to eat when they need healing, and as they have free access to natural herbs, they do not suffer from illness often.

The herbal system of medicine was highly developed in the olden

days by the Chinese, Egyptians, Greeks, Italians, Africans and Indians. The success of these remedies in treating human diseases has had a spillover effect on veterinary medicine, and as a result, several major herbal-medicine companies, such as Dabur, Himalayan Drugs and Indian Herbs, have ventured into veterinary herbal products in a big way. Most herbal drugs used to treat dogs are the same as those for human beings, with a few exceptions. Herbal products have been found to be especially useful in treating skin disorders, controlling ectoparasites, maggot wounds, bladder stones and liver disorders. They are being used nowadays as an adjunct to allopathic medicines by most vets. Herbal shampoos and skin ointments are very popular with dog owners because they are mild and do not cause allergies. Herbal drugs have a distinct advantage over allopathic medicines as they are non-toxic and do not have side effects, and are therefore considered eco-friendly and safe. They are also being successfully used to stimulate the immune system and in the treatment of arthritis. These herbal preparations have the advantage of being more affordable in price than allopathic medicines, and have a longer shelf life.

What are the herbal preparations that can be used for common skin problems such as mange, eczema, dermatitis, fungal infection and pyoderma?

There are several herbal skin ointments such as Newcharm (Dabur), Olinall (Wockhardt), and Dermanol (Indian Herbs), which can be used for skin problems in dogs.

What herbal preparations are effective in controlling canine ectoparasites (ticks/fleas)?

Zerokeat, Newcharm and Loamglo herbal shampoos manufactured by Dabur and Ectodust, Ectozee and Splenderm by Indian Herbs are good herbal preparations that can be used to protect dogs against ectoparasites.

Are there any herbal preparations that can be used for maggot-infested wounds?

Hemax Cream, manufactured by Indian Herbs, and Newcharm, by Dabur, can be used to treat maggot-infected wounds in dogs.

Are there any herbal preparations that can boost the immune system of a dog?

Charmaid Tablets made by Dabur, and Immuplus by Indian Herbs, are recommended for toning the immune system of immuno-deficient dogs.

Are there any herbal preparations for alleviating stress in dogs?

Stress Eaze, made by Indian Herbs, is recommended for treating stress in dogs (caused by transportation, bacterial and viral infections, fatigue, and so forth).

Acupuncture/Acupressure and Massage

The science of acupuncture is a highly-developed ancient Chinese art which relieves pain and treats various ailments by piercing the body at specific points and stimulating them with fine needles. In acupressure the points are stimulated by hand pressure. Acupuncture is the oldest medical system known to human beings, except possibly herbal medicine. Its application depends on an accurate and in-depth knowledge of particular points, specific for each species of animals and human beings. Activation of these points restores the normal balance of the body, leading to relief from disease. Only a highly trained and qualified vet can perform successful veterinary acupuncture. In acupressure, the thumb, fingers or the hand is used, and anyone with

some knowledge of acupressure points can administer it without any harmful after-effects.

Acupuncture works by activating the energy of the living body (*chi*, which means life force). The life force (*chi*) flows into and through the body by 14 meridians or flow passageways. As long as the energy is moving freely, the body is in perfect health. When the energy flow is partially blocked, resulting in less energy flowing through one area, and too much in a corresponding area, it results in disease. By inserting acupuncture needles, or by applying finger acupressure on the point of blockage, the energy flow is re-balanced and good health is restored. The meridian pathways are the animal's or human being's tree of life. The Chinese calls the two main central channels the 'conception vessel' and the 'governing vessel'. These run up the centre front and down the centre back of the body, along the spinal cord or the central nervous system (they correspond with the Indian *ida* and *pingala* of *sakti*). The other meridian channels feed major organs of the body, such as the small and large intestines, the liver, lungs, spleen, gall bladder, stomach, kidneys and heart. There are two additional meridians, the heart constrictor and the triple heater. The energy lines also spread out from the meridians into branches or smaller pathways called the *nadis*. They end, in the case of human beings, in the palms of the hands, the soles of the feet, and in the ears, whereas in dogs they end in the footpads/paws and the ears. By freeing the *chi* (life force) in the meridian pathways, energy is released and flows through the entire system of the living being. A free flow of *chi* through all the meridians, *chakras* and *nadis* means good health. By balancing the meridian points using needle insertions, or by external pressure (acupressure), the energy system of the body is brought into balance. The meridian points being stimulated is like removing the boulders that impede the flow of water in a river; removing the blockage of *chi* restores the normal free flow of energy.

Massage and touch therapy have been used successfully from ancient times to relieve stress, muscle tension and calm the nerves. Animals also feel good and like to be stroked by human beings; the bond between humans and dogs is primarily a tactile bond. Dogs respond positively to human hand massage/manipulation, which has a positive healing effect on them. Massage can be specially focused on certain body parts/areas to comfort and heal. Petting and stroking your dog has a beneficial effect both on the owner as well as on the dog. Massaging one's dog regularly after grooming him has an immensely beneficial effect on his general health, and it also strengthens the bonds of friendship between him and his owner. By just going over the entire body of the dog with gentle hands, one can discover any abnormality/health problems, such as lumps, sores, wounds, ecto-parasites, fever, and so forth. Massaging the ears, footpads and body has an immensely beneficial effect but is not recommended in the case of sprains, fractured bones or broken-skin injuries. Do not massage your dog if he has an infectious disease, cancer, or is in a state of shock. Also, do not forcibly massage a dog if he is sick and wants to be left alone; but even a sick dog appreciates loving human hands gently placed on his body. After the acute stage of the disease is over, recovery can be speeded up by gentle massage, which is also beneficial for spinal problems, joint pains and muscle cramps. Massage stimulates circulation and increases lymph flow, and as in acupressure, helps in releasing the blocked *chi*.

How does one administer acupressure to a dog?

Important acupressure/acupuncture points are present on and inside the ears and paws/footpads of the front and hind legs of dogs. Therefore, massaging their ears and footpads gently stimulates the specific pressure points, which has a healing effect on the body as a whole. All dogs love their ears being massaged.

Can acupressure and massage be combined?

Acupressure and massage go together. Massaging the pressure points, helps in treating various health problems; these are indicated against each pressure point.

How long should one massage a pressure point?

An acupressure point generally takes about 30 seconds of gentle direct pressure/massage to release the blocked energy/*chi*. It is better to initially use the index finger to locate the pressure point, and then gently press on it. Later on it can be gently massaged.

How does one locate the acupressure points in a dog?

After identifying the general area, as pointed out in the diagram, gently move your index finger and locate a small depression in the skin; generally this is the acupressure point, which may elicit a pain response on pressing it.

Should one massage a young puppy?

Gentle massage is beneficial for puppies, and it helps in the absorption of minerals from the blood into the bones, especially in large breeds. Massage relieves emotional stress and is very important for the survival of an orphaned puppy, who should be handled and touched several times a day.

Is massage helpful in correcting behavioural problems in dogs?

Massage can be helpful in gaining the trust of and bonding with a dog with a history of abuse and trauma. With regular body massage one

can enhance the receptivity of the dog and modify negative behaviour such as aggressiveness.

Which parts of the dog's body need special attention in a daily massage?

Daily massage of the ears and footpads, which have the maximum number of acupressure points in them, is most beneficial and promotes good health.

What is the exact location of the acupressure points in a dog's paw?

The pressure points are located in the centre of each footpad.

What is the exact location of the acupressure points in a dog's ears?

The pressure points in a dog's ears are mostly located on the earflap.

MASSAGE THE EAR FLAPS

How does one massage the pressure points in a dog's ears?

The dog should be made to lie down. Take hold of the ear between your thumb and forefinger, as shown in the diagram, and massage it from the base to the tips, making tiny circles with your thumb and index finger, as you slide your fingertips over the ear.

BACH FLOWER REMEDIES AS AN EMERGENCY FIRST AID FOR DOGS

Bach Flower Remedies are being used extensively in humans and animals, especially pet dogs in the UK and the US, with good results as an alternative system of medicine, alone or in combination with homeopathy. Bach Flower Remedies are made from flowers and were discovered by Dr Edward Bach in the 1930s in the UK. There are a total of 38 flower remedies, which are now available in Homeopathic

pharmacies in India. These can be used singly or in combination. Like homeopathic medicines, the mother tinctures made from flower essences are diluted and dispensed as pills/in liquid form for oral administration. Generally 3-4 drops/5-6 pills are given 3 times a day.

Dogs have responded with dramatic results to Bach Flower Remedies, especially when used as an emergency first aid. It is beyond the scope of this book to give details of all the 38 Bach Flower Remedies. However, the most important and useful of them all is Rescue Remedy, which is used extensively as an emergency first aid for dogs.

Rescue Remedy is made from a combination of five Bach Flower essences: Rock Rose (to counter terror and panic), Cherry Plumb (to balance intense tension and fear of losing mental control), Clematis (to overcome fainting and coma), Impatiens (to reduce tension and impatience), and Star of Bethlehem (to reduce the effects of shock). It is an excellent emergency first aid for shock, all types of accidental injuries, acute cardiac condition, collapse, and for dogs panic-stricken due to thunder and the noise of firecrackers. It is also widely used for emotional disturbances and to calm down hyperactive and stressed dogs. It gives excellent results in stressed newborn puppies after Caesarean or Forceps delivery.

Rescue Remedy should be given as 4-5 drops mixed in a teaspoon of water. However, in an emergency it can be administered directly into the mouth without diluting with water. Rescue Remedy can also be applied externally on all types of injuries. It gives even better results when administered with Arnica 200 in case of physical trauma and shock. Rescue Remedy works very well for all types of insects/animal bites when applied directly on the site of the bite, and combined with oral administration.

Rescue Remedy can also be used in chronic skin conditions with intense itching and to calm down over-aggressive dogs, provided it is used continuously for some time.

Dr D.S. Vohra has done pioneering work in India on the use of Bach Flower Remedies and has written several books on the subject.

In conclusion, I would like to reiterate that keeping a dog is one of life's greatest pleasures. Countless people throughout the world have had their lives miraculously transformed and immeasurably enriched by their loving and close relationship with their dogs. Scientific studies have also proved conclusively the benefits of human-canine bonding, as elaborated in this book.

Dog owners are becoming more and more aware of their responsibilities towards their pets, and the number of first-time dog owners is also rapidly growing. They have numerous unanswered questions about the various aspects of dog care and responsible ownership. This question-answer book is meant for all those people. I hope it will clear their doubts and answer their questions about how to take care of their dogs, keep them healthy and happy (they deserve only the best and plenty of love and tender loving care), and derive a joy beyond words from their wonderful relationship with their un-demandingly loving and loyal 'best friends'.

Notes

Notes

Notes

Notes

Notes

Notes